Face to Face
with
God

Face to Face with God

My Best Friend

Terri L. Moore

Face to Face with God
Copyright © 2016 by Terri L. Moore
All Rights Reserved.

Published by Terri L Moore and Team
Terri@terrimooreandteam.com

ISBN: 9781724144485

Contents

Testimonials		vii
Foreword		xiii
Acknowledgements		xv
Introduction		xvii
Chapter 1	Making Peace with Your Past	1
Chapter 2	Let It Go! Let It Go!	17 (21)
Chapter 3	Thriving or Just Surviving	51 (65)
Chapter 4	A Breakthrough to a Beautiful Vision	61 (79)
Chapter 5	Power in Forgiveness	73 (93)
Chapter 6	The Crazy Prayer Warrior	89 (115)
Chapter 7	God, Bless Me Indeed and Enlarge My Territory	109 (141)
Chapter 8	Will the Real Me Please Stand Up!	121 (155)
About the Author		139 (175)

Testimonials

My wife has an amazing connection with God that allows her to connect with people. She helps individuals to work through obstacles that may hinder them from finding their true selves. This book will inspire you to understand how a close connection with God will help to change your life.

—Scott W. Moore

Terri has the ability to inspire others and change lives due to all she has experienced in her life. She is very passionate around helping others, empowering them with the resources to make great changes in their lives. Through the trials of life that Terri has faced over the years, her faith was severely tested, which drove her to pray much. Terri grew in her confidence through her reliance on God through prayer. Terri has become known as a prayer warrior and a woman of great faith, so when she speaks, it is very evident that she is not relying on herself, but on God.

—Renaye Frazier

When Terri shares about her personal struggles, everyone stops to listen. Terri has always been a prayer warrior and I know that I can depend on her to give me righteous advice.

I know you will appreciate her perspective in this book and get ideas to grow in your trust in God.

—Linda Boyer

Terri has always been, and continues to be, a hero of true faith by her trust and life with God. Jesus commended the Roman centurion to the people, "I have not seen faith like this in all Israel!" So I say, we all need to imitate this faith that my dear friend has been blessed with and encourage her to continue in the path God has led her to by helping change the lives of many, both now, and in the years ahead.

—Mark Radina

Through good times and challenges, Terri has been an inspiration by her trust and intimacy with God. She is an example of a woman of faith who is not afraid to pray big prayers, wait for God to answer, then be up for whatever challenge He has for her. Terri has taught me so much about God's amazing love and I'm proud to call her my spiritual mom.

—Allison Spaeth

With Terri as my coach, I have had many breakthroughs in my life. First and foremost, I am having breakthroughs in my relationship with Christ! I am learning to love and accept myself. Terri has an incredible gift of helping me dig deeper into who I really am. I am finally starting to find and love myself again. Terri has a wonderful sense of humor and will place anyone at ease no matter what the topic will be. She has saved my life, my marriage, and my career.

—Jessica Harrison, Executive District Manager, Arbonne International LLC

When I became a Christian 25 years ago, Terri was an invaluable friend who continually challenged me to enlarge my view of God. There is a reason Terri is a dreamer and has touched the hearts of many. Terri is known to have a powerful prayer life and her prayers are filled with worship, thanksgiving, and child-like requests. I am always inspired that she has the boldness to pray vulnerable and specific prayers and then to wait on God to provide the answers. I am excited for this book because I know God has healed Terri and given her so much to share with others.

—Roger Bolender

Terri does a great job cutting to the chase of challenges and issues we face that are unique to a group or the challenges we face each day. She also gives helpful information and ideas on solutions. I would highly recommend her as a speaker.

—Linda Westrick, Area Manager, Arbonne International LLC

Terri is a woman who speaks from her heart and her experiences. She is a woman who has overcome much adversity and truly loves helping other individuals overcome their adversities. It's evident that she is passionate about what she does. Terri's motivational speaking displays upon her ability to relate to her audience. She is honest and vulnerable while being professional and relevant to her topic. She will touch you and move you to become a better version of yourself. She will move you to find true intimacy with God.

—Carla Martin

Terri's life journey is one that is so rich in transforming situations that she is able to relate to many people dealing with the throws of life. She helps each person see the inner beauty in themselves and uncover the roots of sadness, guilt and un-forgiveness so as not to be hampered by life's toils, but able to carry on with joy in our purpose and calling. I know all of us will enjoy reading this book.

—Cathy Bedel

Terri has helped me to find the real me in our breakthrough coaching sessions. She really listens to what you have to say and then helps you take that information to use it for God's glory. She truly has a gift of seeing what your true potential can be. She will help you regain your intimacy with God. Her book is much needed in the world.

—Cindy Lester-Smith

During my time as Terri's client, she helped me improve my whole outlook on myself, life, and my business. I have wonderful keys to continue to move forward and not let my past keep me stagnant. My relationships with my friends and family have improved tremendously. She is very professional, yet down to earth and relatable. If you need any type of coaching, business, sales, or self, I would recommend Terri.

—Tiana Mattysse

I attended Terri's Forever Free Forgiveness Seminar and was uplifted and positively impacted by Terri's stories about her past and how she worked through negative triggers to find her true self and potential. The workshop was entertaining and Terri's speaking style is engaging and funny, but also touching and uplifting. She definitely captured my attention and providing tangible exercises for me to take home and work through. The entire seminar was well organized and engaging and I was glad I came.

—Dusty Teter

Coaching with Terri L. Moore has been amazing. I have worked with several different professionals throughout my adult life and been able to determine some things that hold me back. However, no other professional was able to really peel back those issues and help me address them, heal from them and breakthrough and move forward despite the issues from my past. After working with Terri, I have a renewed sense of peace. I have a better understanding of how and why those issues held me back and am able to recognize when my "past self" pops in. I am finally able to love the person staring back at me in the mirror. I am forever grateful for Terri and her time and support.

—Jennifer Dotzert, Area Manager, Arbonne International LLC

I am thrilled about the release of Terri Moore's book *Face to Face with God, My Best Friend!* I have been inspired over the last 20 years by Terri's bold prayers, and deep faith that God will answer. Her gifts of listening, and motivating others who has learned, and over have ministered to my heart. God worked through Terri to coach a good friend of mine, who had been stuck in life, through a life-changing breakthrough in her view of God and in her walk with Him. So sit back, and see how the Lord will touch your heart and change you through the inspiring pages of her book.

—Kathy Boger

Foreword

We've known Terri for over two decades. In that time, we have come to know her as a woman of prayer. We have seen God answer so many of her prayers that many people would ask Terri to pray for them. One of the best examples is when she decided to start a domestic violence organization for women. Terri prayed for the people, money, building, clothing, support and other items to give to women and she saw God provide it all!! Over the last few years of being the CEO of Beacon of Hope, thousands of people have been impacted because of her prayers.

Terri is also a woman of faith and has persevered through many obstacles. We believe that the obstacle that she has overcome and as a result has inspired many people is the domestic violence that she suffered early in her life. We have seen many who have been moved by her story of perseverance, determination, conviction and faith to overcome some very dangerous circumstances. Terri is a woman who has learned, and over the years, has developed a very special relationship with God. The intimacy that she shares about God comes through in her conversations and she speaks about Him as if He truly is her best friend. We believe that this book will encourage many to begin their own journey to get to know God "face to face," and for that, we are extremely grateful.

In His Service,

Steven & Tresanay Cannon

Minister of Indianapolis Church of Christ and Women's Ministry Leader. Co-authors of the book *Guru Wisdom*

Acknowledgements

With special thanks:

First and foremost, I would like to dedicate this book to God who is my wonderful Heavenly Father, Daddy, and my Best Friend. Someone who loved me when I was unlovable. Someone who believed in me when all I could see was my damaged emotions. Someone who has walked through fire with me. And someone who has saved my life many times over and over. I love you!

To Annamarie Dockus, who has walked by my side every day for the last five months as my editor. I am eternally grateful for your hard work and dedication to me. Your attention to detail is amazing. Thank you for your prayers, friendship, expertise, and time you spent in polishing my manuscript.

To my husband, Scott, for his love, support, prayers, and sacrifice. No matter what type of adventure God lays on my heart, you have always supported me. To my daughter, Lauren, the mother of my two beautiful grandchildren, Bradyn and Zoey, who has always allowed me to bounce ideas off of her. To my two dogs, Max and

Lilly, for inspiring me each day in the office and making sure I was taking breaks.

To my spiritual father in the Lord, Steve Cannon. I am eternally grateful for our friendship over the last twenty-eight years. You have been with me through my ups and downs, but more importantly, you always lead me back to the scriptures. You believed in me when I didn't believe in myself.

To my spiritual mother in the Lord, Tresanay Cannon. I am eternally grateful for you. You are the main woman who helped me find God over twenty-eight years ago. Your love for me has never changed. You held my hand when the challenges of life tried to sweep me under. You have always believed in me. I am grateful you taught me to pray like Jesus many years ago.

To my graphic artist, Karrie McCan. Thank you from the bottom of my heart for your amazing gift as a graphic designer. Your attention to detail is so appreciated as well as your friendship.

To my publisher and book coach, Linda Eastman, CEO of Professional Woman Publishing, LLC. Thank you for your guidance and for believing in me. Thank you for teaching me the ropes as a first-time author. God knew what He was doing when He directed me to you.

To my church family, thank you for always believing in me. Thank you to my clients who I dearly love. You are the reason I love what I do.

Introduction

I believe we need to make peace with our past and learn to let go the things that have been hindering us for years. We need to learn to pray to our Best Friend. We need to fall in love with the Bible more. For, if we are going to have a real relationship with God, we first have to find the real person inside each of us. I think too many of us take God too serious. If this is you, then you better tighten your seatbelt because I am going to show you a different side to God.

My prayer as you read this book is to have many breakthroughs and allow your true self to come out before God. God already knows all the details of our lives and, as Christians, we need to learn to be real enough with Him to give Him the good, the bad, and the ugly. Praying is spiritual work and human nature does not like making that kind of sacrifice. Our human flesh wants to sail to Heaven under a favoring breeze with a full, smooth sea. But we have to work at it.

God wants to have a daily loving close relationship with all of us. He longs for each day to talk with you through the greatest book ever written, the Bible. What does it mean to have more intimacy with God? Throughout this book, I am going to share my journey with you on how I finally found real, true, genuine, intimate, as well as, unconditional love.

Who in your life do you share your deepest secrets with? Most people only share their inner thoughts with those who are closest to them that they trust or people they have gone through experiences with. Do you know who God shares His secrets with? They are the people who are closest to Him. God wants to share His deepest secrets with you. He wants you to know what He thinks about you. He wants you to know about the plans He has for you. He wants to show you things you have never seen, heard or even imagined.

Now in *Face to Face with God, My Best Friend,* I want to help you do just that, and allow God to become your best friend and to be able to speak to Him face to face. I want to enhance your relationship with God in a fun and unique way so that you know you are valuable to God. He wants to enlarge your territory and vision.

Throughout this book, I will share with you many of my personal stories from my life that were awesome and some that were setbacks. But, I will show you how I made it through the many trials to have many victories. I learned how to thrive and survive by letting go.

Also, I will teach you how to pray specifically and ask God for the wildest, craziest, inspirational and life changing prayers you could ever imagine. And, I will share with you how praying to our Heavenly Father can be FUN. I believe that confronting and overcoming challenges is an exhilarating experience. It does something to feed the soul and the mind. It makes you more than you were before. It strengthens the mental muscles and enables you to become better prepared for the next challenges. We must first become more. But to become more, we must begin the process of working harder on ourselves then we do on anything else.

Listen to God tell you how He wants to meet you to show you more of Himself, His will, and His ways in your present circumstances. Throughout your entire life, look for Him. He is there.

To God be the Glory!

CHAPTER ONE
Making Peace with Your Past

"For I know the plans I have for you," declares the Lord, "plans to prosper you and not to harm you, plans to give you hope and a future. Then you will call on me and come and pray to me, and I will listen to you. You will seek me and find me when you seek me with all your heart."

—*Jeremiah 29:11-13.*

"What you think about, you bring about" is a common quote that has a wide impact in how we view our past, as well as how it plays into our future. I am going to take you on a journey into my past to help you out of yours and share the joy that comes from allowing the baggage inside that has dragged you down, to rise to the surface to be washed away.

Finding the future that God has planned out for you can begin when you make peace with your past. Feeling better about yourself in a spiritual, emotional, mental and physical way positively impacts all areas of your life. Living the good life comes when we are willing to come face-to-face with God and release our emotional wounds. This can be hard, but not impossible. Being intimate with God will come naturally as you let go and come face to face with who you truly are. Throughout this book, I hope you can learn from what has helped me to make peace with my past to move on. Over twenty years ago, I went on a spiritual and emotional journey to find my **REAL** self. I

faced challenges along the way. They strengthened me instead of destroying me. From my birth to my 60's, I have found that God really does give us more grace when we let go of the past and find peace in His plan for us.

Being raised in a dysfunctional family is all too common for most people. I was raised in a very negative and unloving atmosphere with alcoholic parents and a brother who wished me gone as soon as I was born. My grandparents were highly critical of me as they compared me to my cousins. They did not love me as we would want our grandparents to love and appreciate their grandchildren. They were often hard-hearted and critical. It was a very tough household in which to be a child. But making peace with my past challenged me to look at my life back then, to forgive them and myself, and move forward.

My parents were heavy drinkers who drank to take away their pain. Dad was a strict and unloving person until he drank, then he turned into a happy and kind person. My dad would get the belt out for no apparent reason and use it on me. I had many days of going to school with welts on my legs.

Mom changed when she drank. She accused me of things and cut me down in every area possible. She spared no harsh words about my hair, clothes, grades, friends and so much more. Her words and actions were all about the fact she felt I would never be good enough.

My brother was unhappy when I was born and made no bones about it. He would try to hurt me and at the very least he would cut me down. He would say I was trash, and no one would ever want me. Despite all that hurt, I still try and reach out to my brother. I am successful here and there, but I had a lot of work to do to get to that point. I do love my brother.

I felt as if I was living in a house with Dr. Jekyll and Mr. Hyde. When you grow up in a house of dysfunction, it can be just like that. I know most of us can relate to that feeling on some level. Most of my damaged emotions came from my family or bullies in school. Negative thoughts were drilled into my brain daily.

I want to ask you a straight forward question: Do you feel, because you were raised in a negative environment, that you could not change to become a positive person? I am living proof you can. Making peace with your past is the start. God and I are your biggest fans and we know it's possible.

Power of Positive Thoughts

Many of our personal issues are caused by things that happen to us, and by what is conjured up in our mind and how it affects our attitudes towards the same incidents in the future. It is the way we respond to situations that shapes the way we view ourselves and the world. Often, we respond out of emotion when our feelings are hurt. The "old video tapes," as I like to call them, play out the past over and over in our minds when situations arise. I challenge you to confront those with a bold statement, "WOW! That is something new I didn't know before." Or you can try, "I guess that was a learning lesson I needed. Glad I passed!"

Our awareness is often filled with random thoughts and unfinished conversations in our lives. Instead of expressing ourselves with maturity and calm, we can bottle up resentment and relive the same conversations over and over again. It drains our energy and takes our focus away from us pursuing our goals. It is like when I had a walking cast on. I got hurt and needed it to surround my whole leg. It worked for a while and I got better, but the day that cast came off, I felt immediate relief. That weight of the cast was okay at first, but as time wore on, it became cumbersome. So, too, can our conversations we have with ourselves.

My family told me over and over I was going to be nothing. Instead, I went on to be an executive director of a domestic violence organization and won awards. I am also writing this book and helping people out of their past to live full lives. So, when I tell you about these issues, it comes from experience.

The way we respond to things that occur will determine the quality of life we will live. While we cannot change the events we experience, we can easily shift our response to them, as well as the aftermath we hold in the future awareness. And if we can shift our awareness, we can bring change to our world. So, I encourage you to shift your language to shift your outcomes. You can choose language that empowers you. You can shift your focus to a different language that actually inspires you and conjures up a sense of well-being. That comes as you make peace with your past.

I have had major trauma in my life in the past, but like you, I also have things happen to me daily that I have to cope with. This is why James 1:2 is a scripture near and dear to my heart. It says, "My brothers and sisters, you will face all kinds of trouble. When you do, think of it as pure joy." As you continue to read on in that chapter, you will see how strength comes from struggles. Be bold and insert your name when you read that.

This is what I am talking about when I encourage you to dwell on language that inspires you. You will have trials come your way, but how you respond to them will be your greatest achievements or biggest failures. When you find the language that helps you most, a shift will happen in your awareness, causing you to respond differently to the world and how it responds to you.

You may believe, or have been told, that you are not good enough to get a job you really desire. Or that you cannot have financial peace due to past failures with credit card debt. Shifting your language can build up your character inside. When you tell yourself, you are worthy and that you are able to be financially sound, you will see opportunities you never knew were out there. You will see them clearer than you did your negative thoughts. Do not let past failures determine your future outcome.

Freedom From the Past

When I was little, I tried to seek my father's approval, as we all do. My life was filled with loneliness, frustration and anger. Since he was an alcoholic, it was a never-ending battle to get his attention.

I played the saxophone because he did and expected me to follow along. I started in 6_{th} grade and stayed with it through graduation. I did well and exceeded everyone's expectations of me. This also came from trying to impress my dad.

I was doing so well that my band instructor gave me the solo for Homecoming! We all know what that means, but a boy in school named Marty became jealous of me. He stuffed gloves down my saxophone bell, so when I went to play my solo in front of everyone I would be humiliated. It worked. I was in front of everyone and nothing came out. I finally got it cleared out, but it was embarrassing.

I sought revenge by sticking soft pretzel dough in his saxophone bell for his big day. It worked, but needless to say, I was found out and to the principal's office I went with my parents. It was awful dealing with my parents. The curse words, accusations and anger flooded me. I was so crushed, cried hard tears, and beat things with my fist. I know my revenge was wrong, but their response was like adding salt to the wound. It was fruitless to think they would hold me and say they were sorry for the circumstances. No one heard me or how I felt. Not being heard is a huge scar a lot of us bear.

This is where making peace with your past ties in to the Bible. Philippians 3:13 says, "Brothers and sisters, I do not consider that I have taken hold of it yet. But here is the one thing I do. I forget what is behind me. I push hard toward what is ahead of me." I absolutely love this scripture and I hold it near to my heart.

Author and speaker, John Maxwell, keeps it real for us and tells us like it is. When he is struggling, he will share it with his fans. He made a comment one time that said, "You have to give up to go up. You have to release to be successful. You cannot climb to the top when you are carrying all the stuff with you." This is sage advice and well worth noting.

I could hold myself prisoner forever to what my parents didn't do for me that day. Those video tapes in my brain will not stop playing unless I turn them off. When I release the past, learn to forgive myself and others, I can make peace with it. If I choose not to, my pain, failures and many setbacks will keep playing over and over. I reached a point when I realized I had to take responsibility for my actions and no longer blame anyone else for my failures. I am not saying it was all my fault. I am saying that it was time I grew up and put the hurt little girl in her place. Growing up means letting go.

Holding things against myself or others was a dangerous spot for me to be in. Since God forgave me, it was okay to move on with Him. Philippians 4:9 says, "Do what you have learned or received or heard from me. Follow my example. The God who gives you peace will be with you." Did I believe that? Yes! But belief is not enough; I had to live it out. Going to the verse before in Philippians 4:8 it says, "Finally, my brothers and sisters, always think about what is true. Think about what is noble, right and pure. Think about what is lovely and worthy of respect. If anything is excellent or worthy of praise, think about those kinds of things." So, I had to not be in contrast to that. Letting go of your past is a personal action.

The Past and Your Health

Proverbs 16:25 says, "There is a way that may seem right to a man. But in the end it leads to death." The energy it takes to harbor anger, hatred and resentment, towards ourselves or others, is exhausting. Every bit of energy should be focused on becoming the person we need to become for God, ourselves and others. If I did not let go of my damaged emotions, it could have taken my life. I had a choice. I decided to live. Life is full of choices and every choice we make will either take us in a positive direction, or it will rob us of the opportunity to pay it forward to the next generation.

Studies show that when we think positively and stay away from the negative past hurts, we experience a brightness to our eyes, increased energy, and our posture even changes. We walk tall and strong. Our voice gets stronger and we are more assertive in our care. Anyone who fights any disease knows that the power of positive thinking can change the outcome for most.

There are also scientific studies that show unhealthy thoughts and feelings can take root in your liver, where deadly diseases can form. We can make connections to our poor health by looking at our thoughts and actions. Your muscles tighten, your heart races, you get ulcers. You can be tangled up and bent out of shape so fast that you could gain weight, creating more health issues.

As humans, we are affected by those around us in one way or another. You cannot escape negative people all the time. But, allowing negative thoughts or feelings destroys you. That person is going on living their life, while you suffer and become unhealthy. That is not limited to unhealthy thoughts, it goes into your physical health as well.

Some tools to stop the unhealthy physical reactions are quite easy to incorporate into your life. Just as we put negative ways in our daily life, we can shift over to other avenues.

Let's take a look at the basics, such as smiling. Smiling more, even when you don't feel like it, can help you think positively. If you doubt me on this, try it next time you're unhappy or stressed. I know using positive actions like smiling have a long-term effect on how I feel after the event happens.

Positive words are another action you can take that will bring back control to you. Use them in conversations with others and in your own self-talk. If you remain persistent in this area, you will find, when negative thoughts pop up, you will be able to replace them quickly. People will marvel at you and wonder what it is that has changed you so drastically. I have seen it so many times in my own life as well as others. It takes practice to break bad habits and insert healthy ones, so be sure to give yourself time to adjust.

Ignore what others say about us. I know that is a trigger for most of us. I know it is for me. Once others realized they could no longer control me, they left me alone. It takes time to change that. Naysayers and gossipers, as well as mean-spirited people, are all around us. So, try to surround yourself with key people in your life that build you up.

And finally, during the course of your day, stop and evaluate your thoughts. If negative thoughts enter your head, evaluate them. Rationally respond to them with affirmations of good things about yourself. Try not to exaggerate or exacerbate the problem. Be realistic with your current situations as they arise.

Christ died so we could have a life full of potential, with dreams and victories. We can so easily mess it up. Living with the cup half-empty serves no purpose. When I feel that my life is heading that way, I quickly turn things around. I boost my quiet time up with God, my prayer life increases, and I go to my happy place- Rick's Boatyard. I love that restaurant. It is overlooking the water and the fresh air does me good. Find your happy place and use it in times of need.

Second Chance in Life

I will never forget during my quiet time one day with God. I said that I was sick and tired of not knowing who I really was and asked Him to help find the REAL person inside. So began my journey to find that person. Before I found God, I was a person who was comfortable cursing, smoking, drinking, doing drugs, dancing in bars and being a professional pool hustler. I enjoyed the look people had on their faces as I took their money from a game they thought they would win! But I finally came to a point when I said that enough was enough. I was tired of being a plastic woman letting no one in.

In July of 1988, I gave it all up to follow God. I was baptized and never regretted giving it all up. It was a battle at first, like anything else. There was a point where I reached my limit. I love Carrie Underwood's song,

Jesus, Take The Wheel. I didn't want control of my life anymore. I had made a complete mess out of it. And when I gave it to God, He made my mess my message.

Shortly after becoming a disciple, I could feel God chipping away at me and revealing my baggage inch by inch. God loves us greatly and doesn't want us staying in the mess we make. He refines us and chips away at our damaged emotions to reveal His glory. Like an onion, He peels back the layers one by one. We cry from some of the pain of the onion, but after it is peeled, it is so shiny and beautiful. Next time you peel an onion, take time to admire its simple beauty after the wrapping is gone.

The Old Is Gone the New Is Here

I think 2 Corinthians 5:17 sums it up nicely, "Anyone who believes in Christ is a new creation. The old is gone! The new has come!" When we walk with God, we can claim this in our hearts. I have seen many people, including myself from time to time, who live in the past. We are the only ones holding ourselves back. God's word is clear. When we are in Christ, we can believe we are new.

When I asked my friends what they saw in me, it was difficult when they told me positive things they saw. I was so frustrated that I couldn't see what they saw. But, that was the way I lived my life. All the self-sabotaging I had done over the years plagued me. If they said anything negative, I spiraled down into depression. I hated seeing that part of me. I knew it well but felt every blow. Constructive criticism or not, it was painful. You have to be in a good place with yourself and God when you ask people that hard question. Hearing the answer is not all sunshine and roses. But, once I became confident in my walk with God, I welcomed the good, the bad, and the ugly. I wanted to be a better wife, step-mom, friend, coach and daughter to God. So, the old had to go so the new could shine.

Thoughts and Attitudes

Thoughts and attitudes do not change overnight. Negative thinking has been ingrained in us and is a bad habit to break but it can be done. Shifting your mind towards positive thinking takes inner work. But as you weigh that out, think through the benefits for you and encourage yourself to try thinking about it, even more so when a negative response would be more logical. Our thoughts and mindsets shape our lives. Taking control of that key.

Even if you feel positive thinking is strange, or even out of place in certain situations, realize that you have a lot to gain in the long term. There were plenty of days over the past 60 years of my life that I wanted to pull the covers over my head and just stay there. But I couldn't live like that. Through all the abuse, heartbreak and loss, I found more strength when I changed my thoughts to positive ones.

My parents, brother and grandparents all let me down at times. They were not often kind to me. That was not my fault. But how I responded to it was my responsibility. Our deepest fear is not that we are inadequate. It is that we are powerful beyond measure. It is our light, not our darkness, that most frightens us. We ask ourselves, "Who am I to be brilliant, gorgeous, talented and fabulous?" I ask you, "Who are you not to be those things?" You are a child of God. Playing a small role in life does not serve this world. There is nothing enlightening about shrinking so that other people won't feel insecure around you. We are all meant to shine. We are born to manifest the Glory of God that is within us. It is not just in a select few. It is in every one of us. As we let our light shine, we encourage others to shine as well.

Mirror Mirror on the Wall

I would like for you to get in front of a mirror and ask yourself these two questions and stay there until they are answered.

1 Do you love the person staring back at you?

2 Do you know the person staring back at you?

I ask my clients these questions and ask them to rate themselves on a scale of 1-10, with 10 being the best, where do you see yourself loving that person in the mirror? It is amazing when I hear the answers. They are mostly around 4-5. This is an indication on how much work we have in front of us. My goal, in prayer, is to get them to a loud and proud 10! God sees us without flaws or blemishes because He made us. He loves us unconditionally. We are the ones who don't love ourselves that way.

When you answer those two questions with a yes and rating of 10, you win! You are with that person in the mirror 24/7/365 until you take your last breath. So, take back the control in your life and work on your love of that person who looks back at you. Become your own best friend along with God.

Genesis 1:27 says, "So God created man in His own likeness. He created him in the likeness of God. He created them as male and female." God made us in His likeness. There was something somewhere that messed it up. Whether it was someone, something, or just ourselves, it was derailed. Get that back now! Have fun with yourself and enjoy your dreams and laughter.

No Turning Back

When I started to find the REAL person inside, it was scary because I was not used to being that person. I didn't know who would appear the next day. Would it be the insecure, fearful, aggressive Terri? Or would it be the kind, gentle, humble, secure, confident and loving Terri that longed to come out. After weeks of working hard on self-improving techniques, I could see the new Terri coming out staying longer. It was starting to actually be fun each morning to see that person greet me. Not only was I drawing closer to myself, but my relationship with God was soaring. People at church were noticing the transformation in me. The little damaged girl inside of me was not in control any longer. I was liking the adult woman I was becoming. It was so comforting to look into the mirror and like the person staring back at me, instead of wanting to shatter the glass.

I saw this quote in a picture frame and want to share it with you, my dear friends. "God said, 'Do not look for me in the past, I am not there. Do not look for me in the future, I am not there. Look for me in the present and you will find me."

It doesn't matter who raised you. It doesn't matter who you think you will become. God lives in the here and now because all He has promised us is today. My success didn't come from who raised me. It came when I made peace with my past so I could live the life God called me to.

1 Corinthians 9:24-27 says, "In a race all the runners run. But only one gets the prize. You know that, don't you? So run in a way that will get you the prize. All who take part in the games train hard. They do it to get a crown that will not last. But we do it get a crown that will last forever. So I do not run like someone who doesn't run towards the finish line. I do not fight like a boxer who hits nothing but air. No, I train my body and bring it under control. Then, after I have preached to others, I myself, will not break the rules and fail to win

the prize." Every athlete exercises self-control in almost every area of their lives, from body to mind. I did that too. I didn't take ownership. I, like so many out there, spent high amounts of energy creating excuses than creating results. Spending more time justifying failures and mediocrities than living up to my highest potential within.

When I coach my clients, I remove negative triggers from their past. Excuses come in the form of, "I didn't have the right parents as role models." Although this could be true, it doesn't serve you to keep that thinking in your heart. Or, thinking you didn't have the education others did, time invested in yourself, not enough money for coaching or counseling. All valid thoughts. But, that is stealing your energy.

If you want to have an extraordinary life, the way God has planned for you, stop making excuses and live. God is waiting and willing to help you. I have a strong belief that you cannot have true intimacy with God if you are not willing to make peace with your past until learning to trust and forgive others and yourself. God will be there, arms wide open, but He also knows we need to be humble. We are not to do this for our own glory, but His.

We see that in people who are insecure. They are opinionated, set in their ways, and always seeking to make others feel they know more than anyone else. So, we have to be humble in what we do, always. It is for God's glory, not ours.

FACE TO FACE WITH GOD

You are very valuable and worthy to have an intimate relationship with God. He wants you to live a long and healthy life. The world is cruel enough without being cruel to yourself. It is a lonely and isolating place to be when you do not know yourself. My mom passed away at the age of 81 from dementia. But, I can honestly say, she didn't know her true self even before the dementia came along. Same for my dad. He was 72 and died from pancreatic cancer. He died a very lonely man. I still love my brother and I am continuing to work on my relationship with him. Making peace with my past is making that possible.

So, do not let others and circumstances dictate who you are. I want you to be a loud and proud 10 and love that person in the mirror starring back at you. Make peace with your past and allow God to be in control of the changes.

MAKING PEACE WITH YOUR PAST

Tips from Terri

Tips for making peace with your past:

1 Tell yourself, "It is what it is" no matter what the circumstances. Acknowledge it, or at least accept that it happened. The more we do this, the more the little child in us will shrink so we can mature.

2 Identify your own emotions regarding the situation. Ponder the feelings of disappointment, anger, fear and resentment. How did it make you feel? What goes on now when you think about it?

3 Embrace all of your feelings. It is okay to feel whatever it is you feel. You are human with all the emotions. You have the right to be angry, scared, frustrated or anything else. With insight into your emotions, you can begin to understand how something from the past could be impacting you now.

4 Recognize you can protect yourself now. You can ensure the event doesn't happen again. Seek and find comfort in your current position.

5 Determine if you are truly ready to let go of your past. Be prepared to release it into the wind and say, "It happened, but it no longer has to define me."

Only you can decide to release the negativity from your life for good.

6   **Live your life consciously in the present.** Staying in the here and now, vowing to live your best life each day, is a powerful antidote to a painful past. Say goodbye to the negativity and replace it in your mind with positive thoughts.

7   **Go after your bliss.** Your bliss is something that brings you joy, pleasure, interest, as well as excitement. Seek out the things you love to do, places you love to go, and people you love to be with. Use your time on earth to fulfill your greatest passions.

8   **Avoid letting anything stop you.** Even though you may still have contact with people who have hurt you in the past, recognize that you hold all the keys to how your life journey continues. Making peace with your past will help you to have that control back.

CHAPTER TWO

Let It Go! Let It Go! Let It Go!

This chapter is for those who need to let go of something in their lives to allow them to have more intimacy with God. If you think you are that person, then this chapter is for you.

How many of my readers have seen the movie *Frozen* by Disney? This is the #1 animated film of its time. The plot of this movie relates to us in many ways. Anna, a fearless optimist, sets off on an epic journey teaming up with a rugged mountain man and his loyal reindeer to find her sister, Elsa, whose ice-powers have trapped the kingdom of Arendelle in eternal winter. From the outside, Elsa looks poised, regal and reserved. Truthfully, she lives in fear as she wrestles with a mighty secret she was born with, the power to create ice and snow. Haunted by her past, Elsa isolated herself. What about us? We are much like Elsa, haunted by our past and trapped under it. Oftentimes, we live in fear that people will find out who we really are. I am here to tell you, this is no way to live and God did not design you to be like this. We need to learn to let go of all the negative triggers that cause us to not feel at peace.

The Power of Peace

"Peace I leave with you; my peace I give you. I do not give to you as the world gives. Do not let your hearts be troubled and do not be afraid."

—John 14:27

No matter what may be going on all around us today, we can still live in peace. The scripture encourages us to not let our hearts be troubled. Mediating on all the negative things in this world can steal your peace. If you have fear, worry or anxiety about anything, then you need to let it go because these feelings aren't from God. He has promised to give you a spirit of power, love and sound mind. There is tremendous power in peace. When you are at peace internally, you can think more clearly. You can hear the voice of God more easily. You'll make better decisions. Even your physical body responds to peace. The enemy knows this, and his goal is to steal your peace. But when we choose to receive God's peace,

LET IT GO! LET IT GO! LET IT GO!

then no weapon formed against us shall prosper. You can live in peace and joy, living the abundant life God has for you.

As I write this chapter, I wonder if I really am at peace. At the present time, I am coaching clients, attending networking meetings, speaking engagements, and my editor has me on weekly deadlines. And on top of all this, I am a wife, mom, nana, and a leader in our church. My car is not running properly, our medical debt is not going away, and I am on a deadline to get this book finished and into the hands of my publisher. So, this is my opportunity to practice what I preach here and now. I need to pray for more peace. I am just being real with all of you. Trying to fit all of this in can cause me to lose my peace, especially when I feel like I am in a whirlwind.

I have had one of the most challenging years I have had to face in the 22 years of my marriage. In January of 2015, we found out my husband had to have brain surgery. Beacon of Hope still needed my attention, but I was in the process of stepping away from it. Then we made the decision to start Terri L Moore & Team.

I want to encourage you that we serve a big God who wants to do big things in your life. You were created to live blessed and fulfilled! You may not feel this is happening right now, but I want you to know it's your time to start seeing things change for the better. I had to remember this as 2015 ticked by with one major event after another. The key to this happening is in that one word "seeing." Despite what the circumstances around you are, you first have to see God at work in your midst. This takes believing and activating your faith.

When you think about your past, what events do you remember? What memories do you allow to play over and over in your mind? In the Old Testament, they had what they called memorial stones. These were used to remind the people about the good things God did in their lives and their victories.

Victories

"Now thanks be to God, who always leads us in triumph."

—2 Corinthians 2:14

Today, we need to remind ourselves to focus on our victories. Sure, we've all had setbacks, but when you meditate on your disappointments and failures, it only drains you of valuable energy. It steals your confidence and joy. But when you focus on your victories, it builds your strength and confidence. It feeds your faith. It gives you a reason to give God praise.

Hebrews 11:1 says, "Faith is the confidence in what we hope for and assurance about what we do not see." What this promise is saying is that before you see it take place on the outside, you first have to get a picture down on the inside of what the potential and possibilities are. This will help you to become a visionary person. I am a visionary in about every area of my life, with the exception of financial debt. I do my absolute best to picture being debt free.

I encourage you today to get into the habit of focusing on your victories. Remember, every good and perfect gift comes from Him. As you praise and thank Him for His favor and victory in your life, He will pour out His blessing on you. He will enlarge your territory in ways you cannot imagine. He will help you to move forward in strength to fulfill the dreams and desires He has placed in your heart!

Have you ever thought about the role of addiction and how it plays in our lives? I've always believed that we are all addicted to something. Oftentimes, when we think of addiction, we think of a person that is considered less than worthy due to excessive use of drugs or alcohol. Maybe gambling or hoarding. We think of it as something that makes a person struggle with a debilitating need that virtually destroys their lives. In my former days, I turned to drugs and alcohol as a coping mechanism to fill the void of parents or relatives who I didn't feel loved me emotionally.

I started smoking cigarettes when I was 18 and got up to 2 1/2 packs a day. I became an alcoholic at age 20. I became addicted to drugs when I was 22. I was addicted in so many ways and felt unworthy. I grew up watching how alcohol was a coping mechanism for my parents. Stress and life would get them down, but then they would drink and be different people. As I look back, they were miserable in life, but the drinking soothed them to cope with life.

I remember the last night of my drinking days like it was yesterday. I was up to 13 Tanqueray and Tonics a day and I didn't even feel it. My body solely relied on alcohol almost every night. When the alcohol was not doing the trick, my friends and I would resort to more powerful stuff such as pot and cocaine. I was so addicted to cocaine that I became a drug dealer! We can all be fooled when we wear masks disguising our true selves under all the pain.

While severe forms of addiction are obvious realities, there are addictions that are perceived as 'lesser' but each and every one of us may struggle with them every day. There are addictions to technology that hold us hostage to our iPhone, iPad and smartphone. It's about needing to immediately respond to that next email, text message or Facebook update (this is all while driving sometimes! And yes, we have all done this). If you don't think you are addicted to your phone, time yourself on how long it is you go without thinking about your phone or looking down at it. Face the facts, many of us are addicted to our phones.

This world is getting out of control with too many impersonal ways to escape. I love getting together in person for face-to-face conversations. But, like the rest of the world, I have been known to be chained to my phone as well. I work on it and try to limit my time. It's a work in progress, but we all need to work on it. Now I

LET IT GO! LET IT GO! LET IT GO!

have a question for you. How much time are you spending on technology versus spending quality time in God's word and prayer? I know I have blown it in this area time and time again. If we are going to have an intimate relationship with God, we cannot schedule Him in-between Facebook and every other form of technology. God expects us to be in His word throughout our day, not just for five minutes. He longs for a deep and encompassing relationship with us. Imagine, your best friend called you and while you were in a middle of a heavy conversation, they thought about something they needed to do and said, "I have to go now." My friends, this is how we treat God often. Too often.

When we wake up in the morning, God is expecting to talk to us through His word and prayer. He longs to hear from His children, but life takes over such as; dishes need to be done, house needs to be cleaned, kids need to be fed, our dogs need to go outside. I have awakened many mornings with good intentions of spending time with Him, but Satan gets into my head and derails me to go do other things. I think God is so excited about spending time with us that He can get hurt when we blow Him off. My heart is aching just thinking about this. This is another breakthrough I want to have this year. I want to protect my time with Him and have extended periods of quite time with Him.

We can be addicted and need to let go of working ourselves into exhaustion to receive perceived prestige and self-worth. I can honestly say, after being an executive director of a fast-growing domestic violence organization and the chronic stress I am under, I had several emotional breakdowns from working endlessly for domestic violence victims. But, I did not throw myself into exhaustion to gain self-worth. I knew who I was in Christ, but wore many hats at Beacon of Hope and that drained me. Anyone who has worked in non-profit organizations will tell you how challenging it can be. This was no exception.

We can be addicted to constant busyness by creating to-do lists, or constantly on the move when what we really need is to be blessed by the peace of stillness. Again, this used to be me. I always kept myself busy so that I would not have time to think about my problems or my failures. I was running away from my baggage that had not been dealt with. Does this sound familiar to you?

We need to let go of the addiction to money, shopping and purchasing something new to soothe temporary pain. One thing that boggles my mind is when I hear a celebrity say, "I am not happy." No money, fame or fortune can make them happy. Take Eddie Murphy, for example. He said on national TV that he was a very unhappy person. No amount of money, cars, fame or movies could make him happy. He had to find himself. But with all his busyness, he still had not found the real person inside. How sad for him.

During the time I have been writing this book, I had to let go of my addiction to TV because I have much more important things that I need to be focusing on. Plus, I will be traveling this year speaking around this great country of ours. TV can be a way of jumping into other

LET IT GO! LET IT GO! LET IT GO!

people's lives rather than dealing with our own. This can become dangerous territory as well as distracting me from my goals.

Some of us need to let go of our food addictions. We can use food to cope with pain going on within us and around us. At a young age, we can learn to use food when we are happy, sad, confused, and when we are angry. That can grow into our adult life. I know for me personally, as I write this chapter, I only had three days left as the Executive Director of Beacon of Hope. I felt I was put in a pressure cooker with so many questions in a very short amount of time. I would go home and the first thing I wanted was to get my gluten-free cookie dough ice cream, a banana, and my almond butter, and melt it in the microwave and sit in quietness until my husband came home. Food addiction can come on slow and subtle but can also hit you like a freight train.

January 2016 was an emotional month for me as I closed a chapter in my life; a chapter that had been open for nine wonderful, but trying years, serving domestic violence victims and their pets. On Friday, January 26, 2016, I had to say goodbye to Beacon of Hope. I had to let it go, let it go, let it go. Many people were praying for me and I certainly felt their prayers. I felt more recharged and refreshed and I don't have a craving for ice cream. That was a good indicator that I was in a good place inside.

How about you? What is your downfall with food? When our food becomes an addiction, it means we have taken our focus off God and we are not letting go of something that is causing this addiction. God humbled me a few years ago because He couldn't stand to see His daughter having meals such as Burger King, Taco Bell, and McDonald's, day in and day out for convenience. I started having brain fog, feeling sick to my stomach, headaches, and allergy problems. I went to a doctor and had tests run, only to find out I was allergic to gluten products. I had to give up practically everything I loved, including the sweets. I told God one night to take me now because I didn't think I could do this. I had to give up breads, pasta, sweets, and coffee. I felt like a little kid throwing tantrums. I even had a meltdown in Kroger's because every item I picked up had something I could not eat. My husband was having a very difficult time with me. I lost so much weight that our friends in my church were asking my husband if I had cancer. I remember praying, asking God to make this go away. I was hoping it was all a bad dream, but it wasn't. It was my new reality that I had a leaky gut from all those years of alcohol, sweets, breads, etc. When I finally surrendered it to God, people came into my life that were going through the same thing and we rallied around each other.

God cares about us on every level. Whatever is causing us to not draw closer to Him, we need to let it go and He will remove it. It is not a pleasant thing to get humbled like this from the Great Almighty. But, it is so necessary and rewarding.

In reflection, I am truly grateful with how far I have journeyed in overcoming my dependency on things that no longer serve me in a positive, powerful, and productive manner. Trust me, you cannot do this alone. You have to depend on God to pull the root cause of your addictions up and into the light. You have to fully trust in God and allow the pained little girl or boy from within to be fully healed. We have to let go of excuses we continue to tell ourselves as to why we can't move forward in life.

Understanding the root cause of our addictions is truly a pro-found revelation. The reality is, addiction is about avoidance. It is the avoidance of memories, feelings, pain, discomfort, current reality, and most importantly, avoidance of our true self. I now deeply understand about what we avoid will remain a constant presence in our lives until we have the courage to step forth and face it. We cannot fix what we do not face. My friends, it is time to let it go, let it go, let it go.

So let us think about these real issues, and reflect on our own addictions. As I shared earlier, I struggled with major addictions. It was not until God stepped in and transformed me, and actually transformed my life, that I was healed from many of my addictive tendencies. This became a deep transformation that forced me to relinquish my dependency on addictive behaviors and vices. It was not until my God stepped in to heal me that I was released from my addictive use of alcohol, drugs, smoking, and TV. Those were all vices to numb deep pain ailing within.

When I made a decision to finally begin Bible studies with three amazing women, it was scary because I did not know God at all. However, when we turned to the scriptures about our body being a "Holy Temple," it changed my perspective of things. It took about two months before I was ready to surrender. We had to work through a lot of my baggage, but then it happened. I totally went cold turkey and gave up smoking, drinking, and drugs overnight because these addictions put my Jesus on the cross to die for my sins. Wow, my eyes were wide open, but not all the way. I left my Bible study and headed to my favorite bar where everyone knew me. It didn't take long to realize that God had chosen me to be in His Kingdom and have eternal life. I left the bar and called my family group leaders, Steve and Tresanay Cannon, and said I was ready to be baptized. That night, I remember driving home praying, "God, please do not let me die tonight and go to Hell." I was scared for my salvation. As of July of 2016, it was 28 years that I had been walking with my God. I continue to do so to this day, and I do not regret anything I had to give up to follow Him. My prayer today is that we can once and for all face the remnants of our own addictions and put this unhealthy dependency to rest.

Fear

Let's talk about **F.E.A.R.** It is False Evidence Appearing Real. It is self-generating. It appears real, even though it is a fear of the future and is not happening now. Therefore, it has no real substance, arising when the ego-self is threatened, which makes you cling to the known and familiar. Such fear creates untold worry, apprehension, nervous disorders and even paranoia.

Did you know that fear is the #1 reason women and men do not know who they truly are? Too many people are living life without knowing who they are. I know, because I was one of those people.

Fear is an unpleasant emotion caused by the belief that someone or something is dangerous, likely to cause pain, or a threat. Talk about danger, threat and pain! A couple examples are car accidents and surgeries. I had a few car accidents that caused me anxiety driving and making left turns. And my husband's brain surgery was a very fearful time. I was afraid of losing him. Then I quickly surrendered to faith. His surgery went well, and he recovered well. I was ashamed of my lack of faith in God. However, I had to forgive myself so I could move forward. It was a great lesson in faith.

We can oftentimes be afraid to find our true-selves because we may discover we do not like who we are. Many years ago, when I began reading MANY self-improvement books, I found myself confused and asking the question, "Who the heck am I?" I have experienced many disappointments, hurts, failures and setbacks from my past such as:

- Dysfunctional family – No affection. I knew they loved me, but they did not show it emotionally until in their later years.

- Alcoholic parents – Drinking caused them to be hurtful to me.

- Brother who bullied – He was sometimes hurtful to me.

- Bullied in school – That started in kindergarten.

- Numerous broken bones – Too many to count.

- Many car accidents – Caused me fear about driving.

- I have been inside an actual tornado – Being picked up and dropped!

- Drug dealer – My addiction progressed to this stage.

- Woman pool hustler – I loved being able to win against both men and women.

- Became an alcoholic – Learning to love being numb.

- Became a victim of domestic violence – From my first marriage and nearly lost my life.

LET IT GO! LET IT GO! LET IT GO!

- Sexual assault victim – By a man with a knife who tried to kill and rape me.

That was the old Terri, full of paralyzing fear so that I could not live up to my fullest potential. I am sure you can relate to me on several of these topics. Jesus died to give us life to the fullest. Many of us are living with our cup half-full because fear is holding us back. Oftentimes, we fear greatly we would lose the crutch of holding on to all of our baggage, because this is the only thing we have ever known.

When I first became a Christian in 1988, I can honestly say I did not know myself. I was buried under all the damaged emotions, fear, resentment, anger, bitterness, insecurity, hatred towards myself, hurt, pain, sadness, depression, and suicidal thoughts. I was a lonely person. I may have looked great on the outside, but my inside was dying of loneliness. I was trapped to the point I felt like I was being choked. I was not living the good life. When my friends would try to get to know me or try to unfreeze me emotionally, I would often say things like, "You don't understand! I am like this because of this so and so" or "I am like this because of this circumstance." We can erase our thinking like this and take responsibility for our actions now. Can you relate to what I am saying?

My friends, my goal is to move you to have faith in yourselves and God, and let go of your fear. I want to start by asking some questions that require you to be gut-level honest with yourself.

- What are you afraid of? Failing yourself or circumstances?

  N/A

- How does that make you feel?

- Who are you afraid of?

- When thinking about your fear, what does your posture look like?

Moving From Fear to Faith

You have to name your fear to get to know it. You can take it by the hand so it can become your friend and ally. Instead of letting your fear get the best of you, let's find out together how we can turn the fear into faith.

Everyone has fear. It can come in an instant and throw you into chaos, yet it can also save your life. Fear is a natural response to physical danger, but it can also be self-created. It can take on the form of the fear of failure, being out of control, being different or being lonely. There is a fear of the future and of death. You may fear love because you fear being rejected. A common fear is being generous because you fear you will not have enough. We fear sharing our thoughts or feelings in case we appear wrong or misunderstood. And then there is the fear of trusting, because you are dominated by self-doubt and insecurity. The immediate effect of fear is to shutdown, and—in particular—to stop any growth occurring in your life.

LET IT GO! LET IT GO! LET IT GO!

When God called me to open a domestic violence organization in 2007, what do you think my first thought was? I was afraid of failing. I had to work hard to turn my fear into faith and I'm glad I did. I do not use the word failure in my vocabulary. I renamed it to a "loving learning experience." As long as you push away, deny or ignore fear, it will hold you captive and keep you emotionally frozen, unable to move forward. We see it in the military, people with PTSD.

Remember times you have met fear and moved through it? I'm sure there were many times when fear arose, but you kept going. Those are moments of fearlessness. Embrace those so that you can draw on them when fear arises, and you need to feel strong.

I shared with you before about being inside of a tornado. I was only 10 years old at the time. I was trying to get back home when a tornado swept me off the ground and took me 100 feet in the air! When the funnel cloud came back on the ground to do more damage, it dropped me about six feet down. It scared me to death. I was in shock for days. Even to this day, when the tornado sirens go off, or I see it pop up on the TV, my first thought is to panic and relive those frightening moments all over again. But then I come to my senses and pray. I ask God to protect me and my family. I pray for all those affected by the tornados and severe weather. I take action instead of being frozen in place by my fear to find safety.

Car accidents brought out fear for me when driving. For many years I happened to be in the wrong place at the wrong time. I had to go through counseling after a bad car accident. I had to turn my fear into faith. I pray to have faith every day when I get on the road. Not because of me, but because of other drivers.

My friends, fear may be close to your heart, but courage comes out of releasing it. Fear can stop you from *facing your shadow* and participating fully in life, but fearlessness will give you the courage to dive into the unknown. I look at my life as the Executive Director at Beacon of Hope and now Terri L Moore & Team and realize, if I had remained frozen in fear of failure, I would not be writing this book or helping others find peace from their past.

I truly believe when a person discovers their true self, they forgive by letting go of the fear that has been paralyzing them. They will become a more secure person who walks around with an air of confidence. They will learn to trust not only themselves, but the people around them. They have broken the chains that have been holding them back and now they are allowing people to meet the real, authentic, teachable, humble and transparent person. They no longer have to ask the question, "Will the Real Me Please Stand Up." Here are a few practical ideas to help:

- Write down all your fears that are past, present and future.

- Find scriptures on fear from the Bible.

LET IT GO! LET IT GO! LET IT GO!

- Find devotionals that inspire you to face fear.

- Pray and ask the Holy Spirit to bring up your fears.

- Praise yourself for those times you did not allow fear to stop you. Make sure to write those down.

- Like me on my Terri L Moore & Team Facebook page, Twitter and LinkedIn, so I can share in your victories. You can encourage others that way as well.

How to Look at Fear through Eyes of Love

I want you to try taking the posture of love. Watch how your body responds as your arms are reaching outward, accepting and inviting. Fear may still be there, but love can welcome fear. It can embrace any negativity. Watch how your breathing gets deeper and fuller. Where fear shuts out love, love holds fear tenderly. It is like the sky that contains everything—the stars, the moon, the wind. With your arms stretched wide, try saying, "I'm frightened" and really mean it—hard to do. Don't deny it, but fully embrace it with God's love and strength.

Shifting your language and mindset will put you in a better place to achieve your goals. Changing your attitude to a positive one will instantly drive away the negative forces that affect your emotional state. The key is to learn how to get more control over what you think and learning to love yourself. I am a work in progress myself. I have not arrived in all areas. However, I praise God for what He has done in my life. He loved me and showed me how to love myself.

I have been on a spiritual and emotional journey for over 20 years to learn to love and accept myself. That year was a life changing year for me as I finally realized who I was in Christ. It is because my discoveries and changes have been so significant to me and my family, I am excited to share them with you. I discovered it is okay to desire feeling beautiful on the outside as well as the inside. I have also discovered I am deserving of caring for myself in a beautiful way because I am worth it. Can you say that? Feeling good about our own self in a spiritual, emotional and physical way, positively impacts all areas of our lives, and I am speaking to both men and women.

I used to get impatient in many areas of my life. I always wanted things to come right here and right now. I could never be patient with myself because of the lack of love I was giving to myself. I would quickly become frustrated with myself, individuals, and finances. I then discovered patience comes out of love. Love for God, ourselves, and others.

Where Did It All Begin

The day I was born, there was already conflict on the horizon. Once the news of my birth reached my 7-year-old brother, he threw a tantrum. He ran off into the woods until my grandparents found him. I was already rejected on my very first day by someone in my own family. Just like Jesus was rejected and was born in a manger, far away from the civilization He came to save.

There was another force at work; a judgmental attitude. When I was 2 weeks old, my mom said he started coming around to play, feed and hold me. However, after he realized I was getting a lot of the attention, he became jealous. That took hold of him in ways and it was a tough road for us. It still is, but we are always working on our relationship.

On top of my brother not accepting me, later on I discovered I was being raised in a dysfunctional family. We didn't know how to communicate without yelling at one another. Personal affection was non-existent. We didn't believe in each other, so no praise was given out. Criticism and ridicule were mainstays in our home. Hugs were for other families, not mine.

Kindergarten is supposed to be our first feeling of independence into the real world in a fun and positive way. Mine was not so positive. I soon discovered bullies weren't just in my home with my brother, they were at school too!

A boy named Jimmy decided to make my school days a living nightmare. My mom dropped me off for my first day of kindergarten and I cried as I said goodbye. Jimmy zeroed in on me. He picked on me about my clothes, my hair and my nose that was broken by my mom while she was cleaning the bedroom. I left that day wanting to never return. When I told my parents, they laughed and told me to "suck it up."

I had to put up with Jimmy for 7 long years because our last names began with the same letter. Lucky Me! I allowed his ridicule and comments to damage me for the rest of my school years and into most of my adult years. I allowed him to shape the image of myself in a very negative way, believing everything he said about me. Even to the point I thought I had believed I had the "Ugly Duckling Syndrome."

I had a hard time making friends because I thought they just felt sorry for me. I had no boyfriends until 5_{th} grade. He had to write letters and stick money in them to prove he loved me. Needless to say, it didn't last long. I was never asked to go to the dances. People in our neighborhood teased me. I pretty much gave them permission to do so because I had a poor self-image and felt unworthy.

Some kids realize they might get teased in school, but not at home. I wish that were the case for me. When my mom was drinking, she would hurt me deeply with her insults. My dad called me names like Porky Pig and Fatso. My brother would call me "worthless" and say I was "no good."

This wasn't limited to my household. Others in my family never seemed proud of me. My grandparents often compared me to my cousins in their achievements. Unfortunately, I had to stay with them a lot because my mom and dad would go out drinking on weekends.

LET IT GO! LET IT GO! LET IT GO!

Despite all the negativity in my family, I had achievements that I am still proud of today. I made first chair with my saxophone. I did solos in marching band and made great friends there. I graduated from high school with a B average.

When I was 5 years old, my mom decided to put me in dance classes to learn tap, ballet, jazz, and acrobatics. I was chosen to do solos at our recitals because my teacher saw something in me that I could not see in myself through all the junk that had been put in my life. Finally, someone believed in ME! I went on to dance until I was 15. I had decided that I would like to become a dance teacher. Unfortunately, that dream never came to be. At the age of 17, I drank too much wine and ended up breaking my arm. I had to have surgery and lost some movement in the elbow. It took me years to forgive myself for messing up my dream.

When I was 7 years old, my mom took me ice skating at the public ice-skating rink. I fell in love with the sport and went every weekend. I soon discovered I could be myself and enjoy the positive energy around me. Due to my skill, I became popular and had friends and some boyfriends. The skating rink became my home away from home. I had people who loved, cared and believed in me. I had a big dream of being a professional ice skater. When I was 16, a talent scout for the *Holiday on Ice* show was sitting in the stands. He saw me and saw talent. He asked me to consider joining them on tour all over the world. I was floating on air to say the least. I couldn't wait to go home and tell mom and dad. Reality hit when my dad said, "No daughter of mine is going to be roaming all over the world. If you leave don't come back!" Another dream squashed to pieces. I was devastated and hated my parents for a long time after that.

Adult Beginnings

During my 20's, I became an alcoholic. I felt no pain when drinking. No one could hurt me while I was drinking because I would laugh it off.

At age 27, I was married to someone who I thought I would be married to for life. After 3 months of marriage he had an affair on me. Shortly after that, I discovered he wasn't in the Marine Corp as he had told me. He was in prison for 9 years for 1st degree murder! Talk about your life shattering all around you like glass.

At age 28, shortly after my divorce, I decided to go shopping at my local shopping mall. It was in broad daylight when a man suddenly approached me with a knife and told me he was going to kill me. Thankfully, God spared my life, and the man was caught and put into prison.

Adult Rebirth

When I was 30, I met the greatest man of my entire life, Jesus Christ. Finally, someone who would never hurt me, betray me, neglect me ever! Ahhh, the fresh air of a new life! Shortly after that, I was baptized into Christ and still remain, to this day, totally His. Christ has changed my life forever. I would like to say I am totally free of my past, but I am a work in progress, and He heals me daily.

At age 38, God blessed me with the most incredible man who I have been married to since 1994. He allows me to be myself and loves me unconditionally. I was also blessed to have a beautiful step-daughter, Lauren, and her husband, Bart, who gave me my two wonderful grandchildren. God has also blessed me with great friends, a great church, and my company- Terri L Moore & Team.

These are just a few areas of my life that have been truly enjoyable. I am a blessed woman today, but it did not come easily. As you can see, before the joys, I had tremendous amounts of pain.

You may have experienced several of the same things I did, like the Ugly Duckling Syndrome, parental abuse, sibling jealousy and such. You may have felt the fear of rejection, abandonment, or being unloved, unappreciated or never measured up to your parent's expectations. Perhaps you have had a failed marriage, maybe sexually abused or mentally abused and the list goes on.

Please, if you get anything out of this chapter, get this- God is a God of love and compassion and you were chosen by Him. "Jesus came to heal the sick and by HIS wounds we are healed." Still to this day, I struggle from time to time with self-image problems, insecurities, and not believing in myself. That is nobody's fault but mine, because we have the power through God to overcome it. He believes in you even when you blow it.

The way to overcome your past is to **STOP** blaming everyone else and take responsibility for it yourself. Did we have perfect parents? Did we have perfect classmates? Did we have a perfect upbringing? The answers to all of these questions are NO! But, to break free from your past, you must forgive those people who have hurt you. As you can tell, I had a lot of people to forgive who hurt me. I carried a lot of resentment and bitterness in my heart for a very long time, most of the way into my adult life, and certainly into my Christian days. I was a very sick person, because a well person cannot live in a negative environment.

Although both of my parents are deceased, I can honestly say I have forgiven them for all the hurt and pain they caused me. I am done with it ONCE AND FOR ALL. How did that happen? Through the grace of God. I came face to face with Him to see how much the sin of not letting go can harm a relationship with Him. It just keeps building walls between you and God and other people longing to get into your life and understand who you truly are. This does not come easy. It takes a lot of surrendering and praying to God to let go of all this junk.

I think about the sad fact that there may be some of you who are reading this chapter who may never move on in life. Why? Because you have a hard time with letting it go and forgiving. When we do not surrender to letting it go, we can become a very bitter, mistrusting, hard-shelled person who most likely will never get to know themselves. I have to admit, once I started uncovering the real Terri, I began to like her. She was loving, grateful, sincere, trusting, and a good friend to people. Day after day, God worked to crucify the inner child inside of me.

Don't get me wrong, we all have an inner-child in us, but it is up to us as adults to control that inner child when he or she misbehaves or thinks bad thoughts. I had to take control of the frightened, less attractive, shy, bitter and resentful inner-child, surrendering her to God to become the person who I am today. This allows me to say, confidently, that I know who I am before God and no one can tell me anything different. When I see things in myself I don't like, I don't get insecure about them like I used to. I just work to change these things. God loves us all so much, and He is not done with us yet. We are like a diamond in the rough that He just keeps chipping away at until we also find the beautiful gem that He already sees.

There is a book I highly recommend for you to read called *Healing from Damaged Emotions* by David A. Seamands and Beth Funk. This book changed my life. It helped me to see through all my insecurities from the pain of my past. God had in store for me to become a better person so He could use my talents and gifts He has given me. When I was stuck under all the negative forces from my past, I did not even know I had any talents or gifts.

I urge you to start today and ask God, and the Holy Spirit, to reveal to you the truth about your inner-self so you can start living as a survivor. Let Him crucify the victim mentality that has been a part of your thinking for way too long. Please keep in mind, this will take work. It all depends on the level of baggage you are carrying around, so please be patient with yourself and give yourself grace as you let it go.

Your Self-Image Affects Your Future and Relationships

Mephibosheth bowed respectfully and exclaimed, "Who is your servant, that you should show such kindness to a dead dog like me?"

—2 Samuel 9:8

Did you know that your self-image can and does affect your future? It may affect you in different areas. You could have been chosen for that promotion but was overlooked because of your lack of belief in yourself. You may have wondered why you are not married yet, or why your friends are blessed with marriage before you. It could be because you are not sure of who you are, or the amount of baggage you are carrying around.

As I shared earlier, all my life I have had self-esteem issues. But, who have I hurt the most with that? Myself

LET IT GO! LET IT GO! LET IT GO!

and God. Why God? Because He made me in His image. When we struggle with this, we are pretty much telling Him, we do not like what He has made.

As time passed, I grew a lot in the area of self-image. I feel great about myself today, but it took a lot of work that year to be able to say that. When you are serious about changing from within, you must get to work.

I enrolled in a public speaking class at my church. At first, I thought this would be a breeze since I had been speaking in front of women while I hosted parties for Home and Garden Party. I couldn't have been more wrong. Tons of junk from my past came back to haunt me.

This was an eight-week course. Eight long weeks. Every week hearing the negatives and positives. The first class we had, we each had to get up and speak about ourselves for 5 minutes or less to get to know one another. As my hands were shaking and palms sweaty, I made it through. Wow, I was so glad that was over. Then, much to my surprise, our teacher asked for feedback. The first portion was the negative and secondly the positive. My heart was pounding because I did not like to hear any negative things about me, only positive. I had a lot of negative feedback that day such as; I sounded like a robot, it was a rehearsed speech and it was not very real. My insecurities took over like a bad hair day. I started feeling very angry towards those people. However, there were some good positives such as; great eye contact, very discipline, and straight to the point. However, since I was already struggling with self-esteem issues, I only kept hearing the negatives over and over in my head. I walked out feeling very defeated.

Week 3 was absolutely horrible. We were asked to speak on one of our favorite books and the impact it had on us. Well, I did as I was told and did my speech on *The Little Red Engine That Could* by Watty Piper. I practiced and practiced every day until I had it down to 5 minutes or less. Going into the class, I felt really great about my efforts. But then, my bubble busted when my classmates started sharing. "You're not real! It's a rehearsed speech! That was a kid's book so it can't relate to us!" It was on and on in that same tone. However, they told me I pulled together the concept of the story to really reflect my own personal story. I was feeling like the Little Red Engine!

After that class, I came home and told my husband, "I am not going back next week!" He said, "Oh yes you are, because I know you can do it!" The devil really got a hold of me and filled my head with a bunch of stuff. However, I did go back the next week. After praying very specifically all week long, I felt secure about my speech. This time it had to be on someone very special in your life. I chose my husband and delivered what I thought was an awesome speech. When it came time for the feedback, I started to panic due to the old broken record. However, it ended up being encouraging and very little negative feedback. I heard such things as; great eye contact, very disciplined, very real, and very heartwarming. One of the guys in the class even said it was the best one yet. Wow! I thanked God and left feeling like I was on Cloud Nine.

LET IT GO! LET IT GO! LET IT GO!

The very last class we all knew we had grown considerably in our self-image and insecurities. My last speech was on what I learned in class. I received a standing ovation and my teacher told me that out of everyone in this class, I was the most transformed person. I felt the victory from within. I had let it go so I could grow and become a better speaker. Letting go of my hurt feelings and insecurities allowed me to have the freedom to speak.

As a result of the class, I am now a better person, better speaker, and more confident than ever before. I have gone on to do great things for God as a result of persevering and staying on track to change my own self-image. I needed it as I worked at raising funds for Beacon of Hope and sharing the stage with Casting Crowns, a Christian band, to raise money for the organization. Also, at events that would put me on TV, or in schools to champion against domestic violence. I wanted to share all this with you to let you know how you can make peace with your past no matter what area of your life you are working on.

I had a dream in 2006, while I was with Home & Garden Party, that I wanted to be a woman that got to walk across the stage to receive awards. Years of watching women go on stage and win only made me feel worse. I did not believe in myself enough to be that woman to win. In 2006, my husband and I finally made it into the President's Club, and I got to walk on stage! My personal sales reached an all-time high. Since I was paid on commission only, I had to strive to be my best because my future counted on it.

> *"When I stand before God at the end of my life, I would hope that I would not have a single bit of talent left and could say, "I used everything you gave me."*
>
> —Emma Bombeck

I believe with all of my heart that we will be able to say this as we truly believe in ourselves deep within our souls.

Hardship subjects people to extreme pressure, and how you deal with that pressure can signal a period of accelerated growth or failure. The hope is that during this time of learning, it is turned into accelerated growth and makes you into a stronger person, giving you an opportunity to forge yourself into some-thing tough, unbreakable, and brilliant. It's your choice whether you take that opportunity to grow or not. You may find an inner strength that you never knew you had!

Patience in Suffering

In 2 Corinthians 1:5-7 it says, "For just as we share abundantly in the suffering of Christ, so also our comfort abounds through Christ. If we are distressed, it is for your comfort and salvation; if we are comforted, it is for your comfort, which produces in you, patient endurance of the same sufferings we suffer. And our hope for you is firm, because we know that just as you share in our suffering, so also you share in our comfort."

Why does God have to keep drilling it in our heads to be patient with Him? In the course of my quest, I discovered I was running away from myself. When I was attempting to speed things up, I wanted to be in control. I am here to tell you, my friends, this is not the place to be. It causes undo stress and it is a hard lesson to learn. Without patience we could not succeed in anything. When we are placing patience in our lives on such things as; careers, marriages, dating relationships, leadership role and our children, we are seeing the true value of patience in our suffering. Our God is wonderful and loves us so much, however, He will keep handing us things to teach us patience until we let go and trust Him.

I have had to learn to let go of many people, things, and circumstances that were controlling my life. In this chapter, I want to share several gut-wrenching stories about my life. This is not easy, but I think you will see lessons learned throughout my journey. As you read this, I ask for no sympathy because these two incidents have made me the woman, coach, and speaker I am today.

My Domestic Violence Story

In October of 1982, I thought I met the man of my dreams at our local Moose Lodge. He was handsome, witty and smart. We started dating and a few months later we married in July of 1983. Within three months of what I thought was our blissful marriage, I was going through family pictures with my then mother-in-law. I stumbled across a document from the courts while she was in another room. Curiosity took over and I started reading the document and went into complete shock. I immediately left her house and ran as fast as I could to a pay phone and called my parents. I told them, "If you want to see your daughter alive, please come and get me."

That document read my husband had been in prison for nine years for first degree murder. He murdered a sixty-two-year-old man he had known, in cold blood. He and his first wife got into an argument. She yelled about him not being able to provide for their baby, so he went to the gas station down the road that he knew. The man confronted him, and he shot him and took off with the money. He had completely lied to me! He told me he had been in the Marine Corp for nine years. My world was shattered within seconds.

That night he came to my parent's house and demanded that I go home before any harm happened to me or my cat. I was afraid for my cat's life since she was at our house. I decided to go with him, plan my escape with my cat and get the heck out of there. Unfortunately, it did not go this way. He became abusive and started

LET IT GO! LET IT GO! LET IT GO!

punching me in the face, attempting to break my arm, and threatening to start the house on fire to kill all of us at the same time. He threatened me by telling me if I left him he would hunt me down and kill me. I was scared to death. No one could reason with him, not even his own family.

Within the next month I planned my escape with the help of a friend who recently rented a new apartment. She allowed me and my cat to stay with her. Thankfully, he had no idea where she lived, and I was safe.

In January of 1984, our divorce was final. It took me months of counseling, support, along with a lot of narcotics and alcohol to cope with all of this. Shortly after our divorce, he married his third wife. We have only seen each other two times since 1983.

My Sexual Assault Story

In January of 1984, I was still coping with the loss of my horrible marriage. I thought I would go shopping at my local shopping mall. As I was walking into one of the stores from the parking lot in broad daylight, a man approached me, and I thought he was going to ask for the time or something else. Much to my fearful amazement, he had a knife and started walking me back to my car. He threw me over my console and laid me down while holding the knife to my throat. I asked him, "What do you want from me?" He said, "A little bit of sex and your money to start with." Then he made me get up into my passenger seat while he got inside of my car. He started my car and backed out of the parking space. I thought I was as good as dead right then! I started coming up with the wildest things to say as I was studying out his frame, clothing, and appearance. I would make ridiculous comments such as, "My husband works inside Ayres Department Store and when he finds my car missing, he will come looking for me. He carries a .357 magnum." When he said he wanted to rape me I said, "You cannot rape me, I am already pregnant!" Little did I know the truth of it....... I was pregnant with my ex-husband's baby, and later on I lost it due to stress from the attack.

I also said, "I recently escaped out of the mental institution." I believe, after that comment, he really did think he was dealing with a real nut job. He decided to park my car in a parking space while still holding the knife to my throat. He ripped my bra and begun fondling my breasts. I said a prayer I will never forget. I said, "God, I don't know you because I have never been religious or attended church regularly, however, I really need you now, God. Please, if you spare me my life, I will follow you for the rest of my days." Suddenly, the man opened my side of the door and told me to get out. He said he was going to drive my car to a parking space at the mall and then go pick up his girlfriend. He said I could do whatever I wanted once I was out of the car.

As I watched my car drive off, I had to quickly memorize my own license plate. I decided to go into the other store and shop around as if nothing had happened. Unfortunately, that was not possible. Instead I had a complete emotional breakdown as you can well imagine. When I came out of it, I had ten police officers surrounding me. Then they escorted me to the police interrogation room, and I called my parents to come. Later that evening, I had to go to the hospital to have a rape kit done. And anyone that has ever had to have that done knows it is a trauma all by itself.

I am happy to say the next day I went down to police head-quarters and identified him in a mug shot. He was arrested and sent up on seven different accounts from me and placed in prison. Once again, the counseling appointments seemed like they went on forever. However, I am grateful to God to be alive and tell my story.

That Was Then and This Is Now

After years of healing from my damaged emotions from all that had happened to me, I decided that enough is enough. I was an alcoholic and a drug user. My life was definitely out of control. It was time to do something to get my life back. I began attending a local church where a friend of mine, Wendy Halik asked me to go with her. I fell in love with the church and I have been going ever since.

After I was baptized, I began studying the Bible with women who had been sexually assaulted and some who were going through a domestic violence marriage. It was incredible to be able to relate with these women on this level. I began a women's group called "His Image, My Image." It was very successful, and women were being healed by God's word.

We can learn to be patient in our own afflictions, trials, and tribulations. Our past, present, and future can suck the life out of us. Making rash decisions during times of afflictions is never good. We will find the success in our afflictions after we find the success of being patient.

On a scale of 1-10, with 10 being the best, where do you see yourself on a patience level with yourself, others, but most importantly with God? This is a scary thought, isn't it? In order to let go, you have to allow yourselves to go to these dark places. This is where you will find your healing. I was never patient with myself. Then one day, I suddenly came to my own conviction; I have been condemning myself all these years for things that really were not my fault. These thoughts of condemnation came from people who projected them over me.

Then – I used to call myself a failure.
Now – I no longer allow this word in my vocabulary.

Then – When I became an alcoholic, I believed I was hiding from myself, and I was.
Now – I know I am free through grace.

LET IT GO! LET IT GO! LET IT GO!

Then – When I was dealing in drugs, I believed I was no good.
Now – I know my circumstances were overwhelming me and I forgive myself.

Then – When I was involved in sexual immorality, I needed to fill the void with love that I never received from my dad, brother, grandfathers or uncles.
Now – I am free of that bondage.

Then – When I was sexually assaulted, it made me feel dirty, guilty and ashamed. I had lost my wholeness as a person.
Now – I reclaimed my wholeness.

Then – Because of my domestic violence marriage and divorce, I felt like I was no good, not worthy enough, an ugly duckling and rejected.
Now – I know the truth of who I am in Christ, a new creation.

After I became a Christian, I still was condemning myself and I had to ask the Holy Spirit to get in there and clean this up. You see the end result as I let it go, let it go, let it go.

Guidelines from God

I have put together some guidelines from God to you that are promises you can hang onto in times of trouble, change and strife.

This is God speaking to your heart.

- **Changes** – Effective immediately, please be aware that there are changes you need to make in your life. These changes need to be completed in order that I may fulfill my promises to you and grant you peace, joy and happiness in this life. Know I am with you every step of the way. Let change come and go through our work together.

- **Worry** – Life and people have dealt you many blows. This can lead to dwelling on your past. Have you forgotten why I chose you? Have you forgotten that I am here for you? Please, do not worry over things that come your way. For today has enough trouble of its own. Let worry go.

- **My List** – Something needs to change in your character? Something you need to surrender to Me with your past? Someone you need to forgive? Things not going as well as you would like in your marriage, with your kids, your job, or your finances? Put it all on My List. Please, surrender it to Me because I love you and I can take care of anything you put into My hands. I take care of things for you that you never even realize. So let it go onto My list and off of yours.

- **Trust Me** – Once you've given your burdens to Me, leave them with Me. Trust in Me and have the faith that I

LET IT GO! LET IT GO! LET IT GO!

will take care of all your needs, your problems, and your trials. I want to help you. Let it go and trust me with all your burdens.

- **Leave It Alone** – Don't wake up one morning and say, "Well, I'm feeling much stronger now. Thanks God, I think I can handle things from here." Don't rely on yourself. Why do you think you are feeling stronger now? It's simple. You gave Me your burdens and I'm taking care of them. I also renewed your strength and covered you in My peace. Do you know that if I give you these problems back, you would be right back where you started? Let them go and leave them with me.

- **Talk to Me** – I want you to forget and forgive a lot of things that are making you crazy. I need to be in conversation with you often. I love you and I want to hear your voice. I want you to include me in the things going on in your life; your friends, your job, your finances, your marriage, your kids, etc... Prayer is simply you having a conversation with me. I want to be your dearest Best Friend. So let go of holding it in and talk to me.

- **Have Faith** – I see a lot of things from up here that you can't see from where you are. Have faith in Me that I know what I'm doing. Trust Me that I will continue to care for you, watch over you, and meet your needs. You only have to trust Me. Although I have a much bigger task than you, I want you to focus only on your part. Have faith that I have My part. Let go and have faith in Me, your Best Friend.

LET IT GO! LET IT GO! LET IT GO!

Tips from Terri

- Learn from your experience.

- Tame down your inner child, take back the control.

- Make a list of the baggage from your past you are carrying around.

- Stop being the victim.

- Don't let negative thoughts cloud your mind.

- Watch the movie Frozen.

- Pray to God He will dig up the things you need to let go of.

CHAPTER THREE
Thriving or Just Surviving

Why do some people bounce back from adversity and misfortune while others fall apart? Let us find out together which character strengths make the difference and serve us the best. Our goal is to become a resilient person who thrives rather than just survive. Success comes to those who have the confidence to win at having a strong thriving mentality.

Friends look at me like a cat with nine lives. I have been in many near-death experiences one too many times and always landed on my feet. Is it easy? No way! But each time I get stronger and stronger. Trauma and misfortune can make a person resilient, or it can allow them to live with bitterness, resentment, and a "poor me" attitude. I have lived them both.

I could never figure out why I was bullied so much in elementary school through high school. It was to prepare me to coach women and men out of the past with bullies who projected negative triggers on them. I didn't know why I had to go through feelings of unworthiness. I am more compassionate to my clients who suffer through this as well. Why did I have to go through a domestic violence situation or sexual assault? I see where God has put me to help those victims become victorious over those deeply traumatizing events.

I was devastated after these things happened to me. I questioned my future. I had plenty of reasons to sink into deep depression and stay there. I did for a time. Thank God above I didn't stay there. He helped me find the strength to deny drugs and alcohol to be a determined whole woman.

I know my God helped me achieve some great accomplishments. I found a lasting love with my husband, Scott. I became the founder and executive director of a domestic violence organization, one that is still thriving today. I am writing this book to help others. But my greatest accomplishment was me finding God. I found Him in my darkest hours of just surviving so that He could make me a thriving woman of confidence.

I want to give some well-earned kudos to my daughter, Lauren. She faced much adversity growing up, before we met as well as after. I have watched her go through heartbreaks and many trials. She is a vibrant and resilient woman today and I am so proud of her. Her husband, Bart, and her children, are her world and it shows. She has not cracked under pressure, but rather has flourished in many ways.

THRIVING OR JUST SURVIVING

Deeply Rooted in Faith

When trouble comes, what and who are we holding onto? Our roots are tested every day. The Bible says in Ephesians 3:17, "Then Christ will live in your hearts because you believe in him. And I pray that your love will have deep roots. I pray that it will have a strong foundation." Strength in relation to roots. We see it all over in the Bible when people changed their hearts towards God like when Daniel was in the lion's den or when Esther went before King Xerxes and risked it all to save her people. That strength only comes from God.

My favorite band in the world is Casting Crowns. They came out with a song called *Thrive*. People, churches, organizations, my church, and I have adopted this theme for goals in 2016. I encourage you to find this song and listen to it. There is so much truth and power in it.

We were not meant to be shackled by anxiety, fear, or worry. We were meant for so much more, and to live life more abundantly. That is a promise from God. If that were not true, then many of our dreams would have died. It is hard for a dream to flourish when we feel like we can only get through each day.

We all get tired and weary, but we have to hold onto God's promise when He says we need to lay our burdens down. Life can beat us down every day, especially with bills coming in the mail leaving us to wonder how in the world we will pay them. Cars that give us trouble and jobs being lost. Or how about health issues? Surviving is for those who may be losing hope that things will turn around. When we are a child of the One True King, we do not live like this.

To get out of the hum-drum of daily life surviving mode, we should focus our eyes on the One who alone, can help us. We need to allow living water to flow through us and thirst for more of God. When we don't, we give Satan a foothold. We were made to **THRIVE** and not just survive. God did not create us to live ordinary lives, but extraordinary lives by digging deep into the roots of our relationship with Him. This helps us understand who He is and who we are in Him. When we dig deep into His word, we reach out to others as we reach out to make God known. Dig deep to find our Father's heart today.

Put on the full armor of God every day, as described in Ephesians 6, because Satan attacks when we are on our way to freedom. I have seen this personally in my own life as well as my friends, family, and clients. I have so many praying for every part of this book that I know Satan wants to hold back. He doesn't want a Christ-centered self-improvement book out there to help people find freedom.

Standing firm with the belt of truth, I uncover the lies we were told that hold us prisoner to the past. The shield of faith protects me from the arrows from the enemy. I wear the shoes of peace as I study on the Word of God to know what will help us. I wear the helmet of salvation to keep my heart in the right place. I carry the sword of the spirit as I brave unknown territory writing this book and serve my clients at Terri L Moore & Team.

Colossians 3 talks about our focus being on Heaven instead of our earthly nature. This chapter talks about putting off things that drag us down. If we think of ourselves as failures in business or not forgiving others, then we are not living into what the spirit of the Word is saying. God wants to use us, so focus on the heavenly things He speaks of. Be a thriver.

John 14:12-14 says, "What I am about to tell you is true. Anyone who has faith in me will do what I have been doing. In fact, he will do even greater things. That is because I am going to the Father. And I will do anything you ask in my name. Then the Son will bring glory to the Father. You may ask me for anything in my name. I will do it." This is really hard to wrap your mind around. Jesus is saying we can do greater things than He did when we have faith! This is hard to fathom and still sends chills through me. I am surely focused on thriving after I read that.

God's dreams are bigger than ours. When we are in the survival mode, our dreams get faded and shrink. Our strengths we once had, turn to weakness. But the good news is, we can rebuild that strength, but only through God. Learn to boast about our weaknesses more than our strengths. I tell my friends when I need help in any area that I am weak in. We can share those with our friends to help lift us up in prayer.

Blessings

Jeremiah 17:7-8 says, "But I will bless any man who trusts in me. I will show favor to the one who depends on me. He will be like a tree that is planted near water. It sends out its roots beside a stream. It is not afraid when heat comes. Its leaves are always green. It does not worry when there is no rain. It always bears fruit."

When I read this, I am reminded of how the trees turn as the seasons go by. In late fall, leaves fall to the ground and wither. This is how it can be for us when we are only surviving in fear. In spring and summer, the sun can scorch us if we are not walking close by God, because He shields us from the harsh sunlight while giving us the actual warmth. Our hearts thrive with color and become strong, just like the green leaves on a tree.

In the song I spoke about earlier, *Thrive*, it tells us it is time for our joy to be unspeakable, faith unsinkable, and love unstoppable. With God this is possible. When we are just surviving, we are numb and wishing the pain to go away. Thriving takes away the wishing and gives us confidence that we are alive and living a good life.

I know this to be true as I look back on my life. Living with a dysfunctional family, an ex-husband that nightmares were made of, and being sexually assaulted. I was truly just surviving from one thing to the next. When I found my true self, I became a thriver. I am still a work in progress. There are still days I want to pull the covers over my head and not care about anything. We are only human. But I do not stay there. I rise up and thrive.

Scarcity Mindset – Just Surviving

I grew up in a scarcity mindset due to my parents always saying there is not enough money for this or that. I would hear my grandparents say how broke they were. I still had things, but they were far from extravagant. I had nice Christmas gifts, the best they could afford. We never went without food, electricity, or anything else we needed on a day to day basis, but my parents would buy a larger purchase to ease their guilt. My brother got a motorcycle and I got a mini bike.

For anyone who grew up in the Great Depression, there are research studies about how that mindset of saving passed on to each generation. It caused a generational curse. It was a time where bread lines were real and people were suffering. It is understandable why they felt that way, but not letting go and feeling secure in what they did have, caused harm.

Most people are deeply scripted in a scarcity mindset. They see life as having only so much, as though there were only one piece of pie. It revolves around the idea that there is simply not enough to go around. If you have worked most of your life and you feel you do not have a thing to show for it, you are living in a scarcity mindset. You are only surviving.

This mentality is also the zero-sum paradigm of life. People with scarcity mindsets have a difficult time-sharing recognition and credit, power or profit, even with those who help them get there. They also have a very hard time being genuinely happy for the success of other people. For example, if you are in the workplace and find yourself getting depressed because someone else got a raise, you most likely have this mindset. This type of mindset can always allow someone to think they are "not enough." However, we know this is not what God says.

The scarcity mindset always focuses on the extreme short term of every decision. What is the most fun option right now? What uses up the resources I have right now so that they cannot be taken away later? We can ignore the long term of every choice as well. The most fun choice in the short term, often has long term consequences.

A great example of this was my mother's dying wish. She wanted her and I to go to the Bahamas together. She wasn't sick at the time, but her memory was declining. Scott and I certainly didn't have the money to do this, but we didn't want her last wish to be denied. So, we put two round-trip airline tickets and a cruise for two on our credit card. My mom and I had a great time, but Scott and I felt the consequences every time we had to pay a monthly payment.

Personal finance is very hard with a scarcity mindset. It pushes us to spend our paycheck as soon as we get it before something, or someone, takes it from you. It can also cause you to be paranoid about taxes and avoid investing. This is surviving mentality for sure.

Awesome Abundance Mentality – Thriving

The abundance mentality flows out of a deep inner sense of personal worth and security. It is a paradigm that there is plenty out there and enough to go around for everyone. It results in sharing of prestige, recognition, profits, and decision making. It opens up possibilities, options, alternatives, and creativity. If you are happy for a friend because they have something you want, and you are also content with your own possessions, that's the abundance mentality.

God has been teaching me what scarcity mentality versus abundance mentality looks like. I live in both worlds at times. I strive every day to change this. It is hard to fathom to be totally debt free. I have listened to endless tapes and read books on being debt free. When you have lived this way the majority of your life, it is tough to break that mindset. By faith, I will overcome this.

I was a worker at the age of ten years old babysitting. In my 60 years of life, I have only gone six-months without working. Scott told me to take six-months off of work to hang out with friends, finish projects around the house, and be a stay at home mom to Lauren, who was only ten at the time.

I pray every day for God to change my thinking about the word abundance. I have always thought that abundance meant money for the wealthy who had plenty. God has shown me that it is so much more. Having an abundant lifestyle can also mean having a roof over your head, a great spouse, and children, great jobs, and relationships. Food on the table and an abundant relationship with God. I have certainly had my own "ah-ha" moments during all of this. If we stay in a scarcity mentality, then abundant lifestyle will not happen.

Abundance mentality focus on the long term. It involves a deep understanding that just because you can't go on a luxurious vacation right now, doesn't mean you will never go. When I see my friends go away on vacation, I want to go along with them. There have been times when I have persuaded Scott to take me on one knowing it would set us back financially. At the time, I didn't care as long as I made it to the beach. Now, I learn to be patient and wait upon my God.

An abundant mindset tends to create positive feelings towards others. It is a source of genuine happiness for that person, because you know that person's perk does not take anything away from you.

Obviously, personal finance is much easier if you have an abundant lifestyle by appreciating what you have. You don't feel the need to spend money as soon as you get it, because you will know there will always be enough.

One of the things I saw in myself when I was only living the survivor mentality was that I was afraid of failing before I even started. I procrastinated most of the time in fear I would not do it right. I was on the road to failure, a road you don't want to be on. Here are several questions to ask ourselves:

- Do we self-sabotage? *"I'll probably mess this up!"*

THRIVING OR JUST SURVIVING

- Do you have a hard time thinking long-term? *"I'll pass over this for now and get back to it later when I have time."*

- Do you procrastinate and put off the hard stuff? *"I'll get to that big project after I finish watching my favorite TV show."*

Let's stop idling in neutral. Grab that wheel of life and drive towards the success of a person who THRIVES. Failure is not an option. We were made to THRIVE.

My belief is when we become a true thriver, we will radiate a dynamic presence, transparency, confidence, security, hope, healing, clarity, courage, and reach our highest potential.

My dear friends, I'm going to leave you with a quote by Mother Teresa to meditate on.

Life is an opportunity, benefit from it.

Life is beauty, admire it.

Life is a dream, realize it.

Life is a challenge, meet it.

Life is a duty, complete it.

Life is a game, play it.

Life is a promise, fulfill it.

Life is a sorrow, overcome it.

FACE TO FACE WITH GOD

Life is a song, sing it.

Life is a struggle, accept it.

Life is an adventure, dare it.

Life is too precious, do not destroy it.

Life is life, fight for it.

Tips from Terri

- Have appreciative conversations focusing on the positive.

- Organize your home and life.

- Share what you have with others.

- Look for positives in every loss.

- Stop comparing yourself to others.

- Keep a gratitude journal.

- Think and pray "ABUNDANCE!"

CHAPTER FOUR
A Breakthough to a Beautiful Vision

Have you been praying and believing for something that seems like it's taking a lot longer than you thought? We can miss God's best for us simply because we give up before our breakthroughs come. Don't let that be you. I want to encourage you that when things heat up and get difficult, it means you are closer to victory.

We serve a faithful God, and He works behind the scenes on your behalf. Your reward is coming so hold onto your confidence, while you keep an attitude of faith and expectancy. Like a mother who forgets about her labor pains when she finally holds her baby, you will forget your struggles once you reach your breakthrough to your vision.

We will take a look through the spectacles of experience to see clearly a second time. Capturing your vision in front of you, while removing the negative triggers that can keep us looking in the rearview mirror. Mark 8:25 says, "Once more, Jesus put his hands on the man's eyes, then his sight was restored, and he saw everything clearly." What we feel is not always the truth. Scripture tells us that the battle is going on in our minds. Our thoughts dictate our actions. That is why Satan will do everything he can to get you thinking in the wrong direction.

Sometimes, it is not our own thoughts that are holding us back. It can be because of the negative things others have spoken over us, and they can become seeds that we can dwell on and can take root to become our reality.

In this life, there will be people who tell you what you can't do and speaking negativity into your life. We can latch onto those words and that can cause what the scriptures call a "stronghold" in our lives. We can break those strongholds by rejecting the lies, forgiving the person, and embracing God's truth about who we are.

As you take inventory of your thought life, ask yourself this question, "Where did these thoughts come from? Do they line up with what God says about me?" When you see negative things are not of God's thoughts of you, you can breakthrough to a clear vision about yourself. I am going to give you a clear of example of this.

When I became a Christian in 1988, I was a very insecure person who lacked confidence. I certainly didn't trust people. I was just starting to scratch the surface of who I was when my family group leader surprised the daylights out of me. He announced that I would be a co-leader with my friend Wendy. I blurted out, "Me? Why?!" I had blurry vision about myself because I had

A BREAKTHROUGH TO A BEAUTIFUL VISION

not had my breakthroughs. I couldn't see the incredible opportunities God had for my life. I let negative thoughts from the past lead me in my words. I didn't see what God was saying about my purpose. Can you relate to this? Even if we do not think we are worthy of God's calling, God does.

I can look back on my life and see when God was calling me to do something great. I was living in my past and couldn't accept that I was worthy or simply blind to it, so I would let opportunities pass me by.

In Psalm 2:3 it says, "Let us break their chains and throw off their shackles." We are marked as Christians, then darkness wants to disconnect us from God's kingdom. We are marked by the hands of God and stamped with His approval. We can be chained to a person, or circumstances, from your past even today. That can hinder us from breakthroughs.

We can get worried about what others think and get upset about many things. Some of those things are completely out of our control. Just look in Luke 10:40 when Martha tells Jesus to have Mary stop what she is doing, which was worshiping Him and loving Him, and help her. Know yourself when you are reaching the Martha level. Laugh a little and try not to take yourself seriously. We allow too many people to offend and upset us. In my coaching sessions I see this a lot. I call it "being chained up." Our only chain should be the Kingdom of God.

Some of us could have been tested by God and truly missed the boat if we would have said NO to God and

YES to sin. We could have missed the goodness of God. How much do we complain about our life? Yes, this a big one for most of us. Serenity and peace can rule some of the complaining part out. I am a work in progress in this area, but every day I strive for a new level. We worry about our health, marriage, finances, job changes, children, and aging spouses, or parents. These things will always be in our lives to some degree. Managing them will help. But, remember we will not have things perfect until we are in Heaven. That is a truth that we forget at times of crisis.

Our stress in life can rob us of the sweet serenity and peace that only the Holy Spirit can give us. He gave it to us the moment we made the decision to follow Him, but somewhere along the line, we forgot that. The song, *Just Breathe* by Johnny Diaz, comes on the radio and I stop what I'm doing to listen to it and just breathe. It helps me to stop and ask God for peace, patience, joy, self-control, kindness, goodness, and security.

Deuteronomy 4:29 says, "But if from there you seek the Lord your God, you will find him if you seek him with all your heart and with all your soul." Dream and give yourself permission to seek Him with all heart. As Margaret Thatcher once said, "Watch your thoughts, for they become words. Watch your words, for they become actions. Watch your actions, for they become habits. Watch your habits, for they become your character."

I say this with full knowledge of the struggle. As I get ready to finish out this book, my husband and I have faced some things that piled up. Our dear friend, Eric Waltz, passed away. Two days later, Scott lost his brother suddenly. He went to Texas to sort through his affairs with his sister. That left me home trying to manage the house, my book, Terri L Moore & Team, and my dogs. The air conditioner went out while Scott was gone, as well as other day to day things. So my thoughts, words, actions, habits, and character were all put to the test. Just like you all face in your day to day lives.

Blame Shifting to Breakthrough

One of my major breakthroughs this year was to get this book done and into the hands of my readers. As we edge closer to getting done, I have had one distraction after another. My enemy, and yours, Satan, does not want this book to come out for many reasons. He will do what he can to destroy my breakthrough. But, I don't blame him for my book not being completed. I have to remember what defines a breakthrough to begin with.

A personal breakthrough starts with a complete mind shift. A sudden, dramatic, and important discovery, or development forward, with success and improvement.

Stay with me as I explain a few things you may not have thought about as a breakthrough before. It is not typical, but you will understand as it unfolds.

Breakdowns can sometimes be breakthroughs that we just haven't seen the other side of yet. I am not talking about nervous breakdowns where you go to the hospital or take medication for it. I am talking about questioning everything, getting tired, having irrational anger, or being mad at ourselves for failure. Satan wants you to have breakdowns. But, reaching these points can be a moment of transition for us, and that is where Satan wants us to be blind to hope for a breakthrough. Let's take a look at what that means.

Questioning everything leads to getting tired, and from that, we are ready to make a shift. Irrational anger can lead us to be angry at ourselves. This can lead us to a major breakthrough to asking God to change that. We get angry and fed up enough, we will make a change to stop the madness. So, having a breakdown, of sorts, can lead to other victories. This can lead to new ideas of philosophy and spirituality. Finding new ways to improve ourselves.

We begin to see patterns when we realize the things that keep resurfacing in our lives are products of what you believe they are or should be. Some are family, relationships, jobs, ideas, finances, and feelings. If we could figure out the patterns and how to change them, then we can change the way they emerge in our lives. We are not mad at the world, others, or God. Satan wants us blind to things and wants you to continue to shift blame on yourself and others. That is what he does best. But, you have a choice.

Realizing there is a difference between happy thoughts and happy feelings is a breakthrough. We have been trying to fill ourselves up with happy thoughts forever, only to find that you get attached to a certain

A BREAKTHROUGH TO A BEAUTIFUL VISION

outcome that is not reality. That increases your unhappiness. Feeling happy will allow you to be happy about the potentials to focus on the patterns.

As children, we experience feelings and fears that can come to the surface. It can feel like it was never really gone. The thoughts, ideas, beliefs, and feelings we kept tucked away were silently guiding our lives. We just didn't know it. A breakthrough is when we decide we are not going to be a victim to any of those feelings. The breakdown starts and we feel a kind of intense mental and emotional turmoil. That is a sign we are in the process of changing. We decide to be done accepting our old "normal" and adopt a new way.

Say you have a million-dollar idea, found a great relationship, or finally the big break came, you can become paralyzed by resistance. Happiness and fear can be perceived to an equal degree. It's not that we are actually resisting our new life, it's that we are very clearly identifying with what we want and experiencing a natural balanced amount of fear with it. It seems like our emotional state is unwarranted. We shouldn't feel anxious or depressed, but we do. Our irrational fears are there, and we can't always make sense of them. We are in process of developing that skill. We can be uncertain about big adventures coming into our lives, but coming to terms with how we define ourselves, based on how others see us or how we should be in our mind, can be the difference between what we think we want and what we actually want.

We are terrified of loss or of losing one thing that we think will save us. Even if it is only an emotional salvation. This is what happens when we begin to realize that nothing can do that for us. We are not afraid of loss, so much as we are afraid of being forced to accept the reality before we think we are ready to give up on things we need to give up on, but not giving up on our dreams, or relationships that we thought we wanted.

There is a song called, *Glow in The Dark* by Jason Gray. One of the lyrics says, "The more broken we are, the more we shine in the dark." We are all broken, every single one of us walking around in this world. This is a great place to be because we are humble. And when we are humble, God can do great work in us. Our pride will hold God back from doing His greatest work in us.

Training to Breakthrough

I teach and train at workshops, speaking engagements, and coaching sessions, that in order to turn negative energy into breakthroughs, you must learn to handle adversity with stamina to come out on the other side.

Assuming responsibility for your situation without blaming others. People hurt us, sometimes deeply. I grew up with people in my family and at school who did not always treat me nicely. I held onto all of this until I was in my late thirties and until I realized it was no longer serving me in a positive, productive, and powerful manner. I was allowing them to have way too much power over me. I had a breakthrough for me to resign

A BREAKTHROUGH TO A BEAUTIFUL VISION

from executive director into the unknown of starting my own business and writing a book. Had I lived in the past, and not accepted my own responsibility for my situation, I would not be writing this book. Nor would I be Terri L Moore & Team, helping to coach people out of their past to freedom. The people around me growing up were not positive about me. But I had to take action if I was going to be more than that.

I had several car accidents over the years and injured the left side of my neck and back. Week after week I would go see Dr. Cooper, my chiropractor. I would feel great, but a few days later it would all go out again. He finally sat me down and said, "Terri, I really care about you as your doctor and friend. I think there is something else going on besides the damage from the car accidents. I think it is an emotional problem." I laughed and said, "Are you telling me I need a shrink?"

He laid me on the table and performed a technique called B.E.S.T.. Bio Energetic Synchronization Technique. It allows the balancing of the entire central nervous system, which in turn has an effect on physical complaints, emotional stress, and nutritional issues.

He had me think about my ex-husband and the hurt from all of that. He had me talk to him about it as he worked. After it was released out of my body, I went to work on a forgiveness exercise. It is so in-depth that I can't write it here. But, I teach it to my clients to help them. It is so worth it. It brings freedom and has changed my life forever. I took back the power, and became strong and resilient over time. I am proud of my achievement. It was hard won, but I did win.

Instead of worrying about our past, focus on our energy to improve the areas within our sphere of influence. Take responsibility for our strength of self, careers, health, and finances. I am taking responsibility for my breakthrough to train and coach men and women out of their past by having breakthroughs. I don't want fear to conquer me to steal my joy in an instant. I know God has great plans for me and each one of you. He refines us as we take the responsibility.

Victimhood

Thinking about thriving instead of being a victim of the past mentality, can put us on a fast track for future success. Those videotapes we have played over and over in our minds, of people projecting stuff in our past, or self-talk you tell yourself, need to go. I am speaking from experience that those videotapes will hold you back until you learn to delete them, or replace them, with positive self-talk. Thriving versus victim.

When you finally breakthrough the tapes of victimhood, you will not allow people or circumstances to control your destiny. God wants us to dream big because He has big dreams for us. I am dreaming big. I dream of speaking in front of thousands of men and women in downtown Indianapolis. Just like Joyce Meyer or Beth Moore, coaching and teaching individuals how to have many breakthroughs. I dream to travel around the

A BREAKTHROUGH TO A BEAUTIFUL VISION

United States doing seminars, workshops, radio shows, as well as TV interviews. I can't do that if I stay a victim.

I am being confident in my dreams and allowing God to refine me and chip away at me to shine the victorious woman inside. I am stronger when I serve others through my experiences. I take only the past as prisoner, so I can free myself from the chains of being a victim.

Are you a business owner or leader in your community and need a major breakthrough now? Are you afraid of failing? People can project failure onto us. Psalm 139:13 says, "For you created my inmost being; you knit me together in my mother's womb. I praise you because I am fearfully and wonderfully made; your works are wonderful; I know that full well. My frame was not hidden from you when I was made in the secret place, when I was woven together in the depths of the earth. Your eyes saw my unformed body; all the days ordained for me were written in your book before one of them came to be. How precious to me are your thoughts, God! How vast is the sum of them! If I were to count them, they would outnumber the grains of sand. When I awake, I am still with you."

When I read this, it really did change my perspective of myself. God does not think of me as a failure, rather He sees me as His perfect creation. Realizing this convicted me about thinking of myself as a failure. No matter who told me that in the past, God tells me that in His word. So, when you have a big dream, relationship, or job to pursue, step out in faith and know God has this.

He made you perfect for His purposes. He will show you the way.

When I coach clients, I have them do a negative emotional chart. I included some of the words in the back of this book. It has over 100 negative emotions that could be going on in our minds, heart, and soul. I ask them to circle the ones that apply to themselves after listening to their story. This helps me gauge where to start. It is painful. But, the Holy Spirit needs to bring up these "garbage" emotions so we can have breakthroughs. It takes a willingness, but we all want the breakthrough.

I have clients who are in direct sales who long to have breakthroughs in their careers. They wanted to be in the corporate world but realized that the past was holding them back. Breakthroughs were not there. I am so proud of them for the hard work they went through, because many of them are soaring. It is a beautiful thing to see a breakthrough open a vision. They have let go and are doing great things for themselves, their families, business, and God.

One of the things I learned when I was working through my past was that we cannot have visions if we are looking in the past. They won't be clear. People call me the crazy visionary because I was so excited when I had my breakthroughs. They allowed me to have vision beyond the norm.

Next time you are in your car, look in the rearview mirror for five minutes. Think about your past and what could be making it blurry for you today. Then stare into

A BREAKTHROUGH TO A BEAUTIFUL VISION

the windshield for five minutes. Write down what this looks like and what you see for your future.

Take a blank piece of paper and draw two large circles next to each other. List out who you think you are today. The other side you list who you want to be.

Tips from Terri

- Every day repeat this statement, "I willingly and lovingly release and let go of all things that no longer serve me in a powerful, productive, and positive manner."

- Ask God today who is working behind the scenes on your behalf to give you deep faith, until you see every beautiful breakthrough from your past become a vision.

- Ask God to reject negative triggers and lies from your past.

- Pray for every stronghold to be broken.

- Optional – Take a roll of saran wrap and secure it from top to bottom on a door frame. When it is secured, bust through it to the other side. This is what a breakthrough feels like.

- A MUST DO! Take the negative chart provided for you and circle everything you feel people have projected over you in your past. Include yourself.

You Can Do This, I Believe in You!

CHAPTER FIVE

Power in Forgiveness

When you think about your past, what events do you remember? What memories of people who have hurt you do you allow to play over and over in your mind? We have all done this at one time or another.

Being rooted in faith will allow you to forgive. It takes great faith in God, and ourselves, to be able to forgive people that have hurt us. Your faith will allow you to surrender to no longer being enslaved to sin and their actions no longer controlling your life. Growing in forgiveness is growing in faith. Jesus forgave my sins when He offered me grace and mercy, which He has for you as well.

Forgiveness brings about miracles in our lives. I know forgiving others was the greatest decision I made. I had a lot of people to forgive, but when I made the choice to let go of it, I was free. You have the chance to make that choice as well. It is yours alone to make. No one can force you into it. Even God will not force you to forgive. But, He gives us the example when His son hung on the cross. So, take it in and think about it for a moment Life with God is not meant to be at a standstill.

When we do not forgive others, it is sin. We know that sin destroys our vision for our life. Anyone can hold a grudge, but it takes a person with **character** to forgive. When we do, we release ourselves from a painful burden. Forgiving doesn't make what happened to you okay. And it certainly doesn't mean that person has a place in your life. It just means you have made peace with pain and are ready to let go and move on.

My belief is when someone learns how to forgive and go through the process, they will begin to see themselves blossom and learn to feel secure with who they are. They will die to their old self, patterns, and habits, and will learn to be radiant and secure. They will no longer be paralyzed by hurt and fear, but rather walking around in confidence and trusting others again.

Breaking those chains that have held us back, people will see the teachable, humble, and transparent person we really are. I know this first hand when I finally forgave my ex-husband for all the wicked things he did to me. I was able to have compassion for him. Yes, real compassion. I saw him a number of years ago at his brother's funeral. When he saw me, he hugged me so tight, I thought my neck would break. I didn't feel negative feelings and I knew then and there I had moved on. I was a transparent person to those around me. Humble and teachable by God.

Forgiveness involves letting go. Jesus shows us this in Luke 23:34 when He says, "Father, forgive them, for they do not know what they are doing." He wanted to go forth in power. He had to let go.

POWER IN FORGIVENESS

Remember playing tug of war as a child? I loved that game. As long as you held onto that rope you were in a war. When someone has let go, the war is over. When you forgive your parents, siblings, bullies, relatives, and ex-spouses, you are letting go of your end of the rope. No matter how hard they tug on the other end, if you have released your end, the war is over for you.

Robert Muller once wrote,

> *"To forgive is the highest, most beautiful form of love. In return, you will receive untold peace and happiness, forgiveness and free-dom. Everybody longs for it, but true freedom is available only by making peace with your past along with the help of our Heavenly Father. A profound, life changing experience."*

As a breakthrough coach, I teach clients a giant step to spiritual maturity is overcoming bitterness and resentment. You can't for-give when you have bitterness and resentment in your heart. I devote a lot of time to this one area with my clients.

Poison

In Ephesians 4:31-32 is says, "Get rid of all bitterness, rage and anger, brawling and slander, along with every form of malice. Be kind and compassionate to one another, forgiving each other, just as in Christ, God forgave you."

Bitterness and resentments are poisons that destroy our lives. We have all been hurt or caused hurt to someone else. When we get hurt, we want to retaliate and hurt them for hurting us, but we usually end up hurting other people in the process. We all know the saying, "Hurt people, hurt people." We see it played out daily in our lives and on TV.

Sadly, we can become the thing we dislike in someone else if we do not forgive and let go of bitterness and resentment. People who have been cheated on, usually cheat on others. If we have been abused, we could possibly abuse others. When we are bitter, it can move into hate, which is akin to a heart to murder someone out of anger. And that is not a stretch. Just listen to the news.

I have heard this story over and over while serving the domes-tic violence community. Hate is a very strong emotion, and I cringe when I hear it come out of anyone's mouth. It can be towards others or themselves. It is a dangerous area to be in and can lead to suicide. I know, I have been there myself.

I once knew a woman who was sexually abused by her father, and later raped. As one can imagine, sexual abuse and rape are very painful areas and lead to other issues. Out of her bitterness and resentment came the inability to forgive. She became sexually promiscuous in an effort to punish men for the pain she held inside. The last time we spoke several years ago, she said she had been with over 65 men, and over half were within a six-month period, when she was in deep resentment and anger. She associated her pain with men and used them accordingly. Who was most hurt by all of this? She was.

I am a firm believer that our pain is 90% self-inflicted as a result of the things that have happened to us and around us. We should look at our motives for wanting people in our lives and if they are healthy. We can attract the wrong people because our motives are selfish. Even when they are pure, we still may need to heal from the past pain and unresolved issues. Then we can learn to be happy alone and love ourselves, so we can love others around us.

Release and Overcome

God has given you the authority to set yourself free and release yourself from bitterness and pain. Allowing the injustice of others causes you to miss out on God's best plans for you. I know first-hand how hard this is. I've cried many tears into my pillow until I thought it would float away. I deeply understand disappointment, pain, and struggling to forgive myself and others that have hurt me. Walking around angry and bitter causes you to live in pain daily. You will not reap happiness and peace that way.

Let us take a look at ten ways to overcome bitterness and resentment. These may seem like common sense, but they require our co-operation with God to accomplish.

So walk with me through these steps and see what we can do to come out of the chains.

First step involves asking God to forgive you for being bitter and resentful. Then ask Him to forgive those who have hurt you. I know this can be difficult for us sometimes. But, we see the answer in the Bible in Matthew 6:14 where it says, "For if you forgive people when they sin against you, your Heavenly Father will also forgive you. But if you do not forgive others their sins, your Father will not forgive your sins."

Secondly, do not allow the bad that has happened to keep you from God's best. Satan loves to keep us in that mindset. All the bad I went I through held me hostage long enough. I had more for God to use me for, than sitting in dark anger.

Third, as you work your way out of the bitterness and resentment, resist the temptation to start a relationship with someone. You could possibly hurt someone else, inadvertently, and also cause yourself more hurt. We are built for relationships, but during this time we are focusing on getting help. Find someone to help you be accountable in this area.

Fourth step deals with daily prayer and researching scriptures to study and apply to daily life. Find a Bible with a concordance, or use the electronic version, and search for words connected to your issues. Write them down and keep them handy for times when those feelings surface, because they surely will. I have key verses to my life's story that have blessed me when I was at a low point.

POWER IN FORGIVENESS

Fifth is realizing God will bring you justice. You are to forgive. He said in Romans 12:19, "I am the One who judges people. I will pay them back." The God we serve fights for us. We need only be still.

The sixth step shows us forgiving removes the offender's power to hurt us. I could let my ex-husband's abuse rule me. But, I chose to let it go. He no longer controls my thoughts or feelings. Sometimes we have to seek professional help for this necessary action.

Seven is about understanding what walking around in bitterness and resentment does to us as well as the other person. They live their lives in enjoyment. You are walking around in pain and anger. You are slowed down in your days and facing depression. They may even know you are in pain and they are delighted, depending on the condition of their soul. Or, you are the only one who knows and left twisting. So take back enjoyment.

Eight is allowing God to help you to forgive and forget. Some of us don't know if God will do that or not, so we live in constant fear and pain. But, Matthew 5:44 says, "But I tell you, love your enemies and pray for those who persecute you." It is a command by God to do that. He has forgiven us and has tossed our sin as far as the east is from the west. Can we do the same? I had to in order to be free. I trusted Him to do what He promises and have not been sorry.

Nine is about not reliving what has happened when you for-give. You are free of it, so do not play that over and over in your mind. If it comes up, recognize it and then ask God to take it away from your memory. It serves no purpose. I saw that with my own sexual assault. It is easy to relive the nightmare. It is far more comforting to ask God to take it away so I can live my days healthy and happy.

Lastly, stay rooted in the Bible. It will guide you and give you examples every day on how to live fully and free of the sin of not forgiving those that have hurt you. God knows the pain. He knows mine. But, when I read His word, I step out of it and live happy.

God forgives us time and time again. In Colossians 3:12-13 it says, "Therefore, as God's chosen people, holy and dearly loved, clothe yourself with compassion, kindness, humility, gentleness, and patience. Bear with each other and forgive one another if any of you has a grievance against someone. Forgive as the Lord forgives you."

Before we get to the beauty of what forgiving looks like, let us take a look at what an unforgiving heart looks like, as well as what affect it plays in our lives.

The Unforgiving Heart

With an unforgiving heart, it may affect your physical body. Migraines, arthritis, heart health, less energy, and cancers. The stress is enough to send us into a tailspin. If you look in the back of this book at the negative emotional healing chart, you will see over 100 negative words people can use about themselves and others. An unforgiving heart can damage our emotions through fear, pain, anger, bitterness, and refusing to accept the reality of our situations. In turn, that will affect any illness we experience to bring us further down.

Deadening part of your heart leads to lack of joy, love, peace, feeling rested, and future possibilities. The energy you spend on not forgiving others, affects all of those wholesome attributes that we strive for in life. It can lead to bondage and torments, leaving you in a prison.

Learning to forgive yourself can lead to achieving a better life for you and others around you. James 2:8 says, "If you really fulfill the royal law according to the scriptures, 'You shall love your neighbor as yourself.'" When we don't follow this way of life, we find we have trouble loving others. A critical part of starting your healing process to finding the real person inside deals with this issue. I struggled for many years with this due to others pounding negative words into my brain. It kept me feeling stuck in a negative tunnel, spinning, and getting nowhere.

I'm sure most of us that deal with unforgiving hearts have said statements about ourselves that were hard. How about, "Stupid idiot!" and "Way to go, stupid!" We can hear our voice as we read, "No wonder no one likes me." The list goes on and on. These are all signs of lacking in forgiveness toward yourself. I knew these well until I learned the freedom of forgiveness. If I come close to saying anything negative about myself, I quickly stop and forgive myself as I move on.

A perfect example of negative self-talk comes from a long time ago, when I didn't have much confidence in myself. I had a presentation to do in front of high-profile people. I was so nervous I sprayed window spray on my hair instead of hairspray! Needless to say, my hair was sticky, shiny, and I couldn't get a comb or brush through it to save my life. I started to yell at myself saying, "Now you look uglier than you did before!" Do you think my presentation went well? Absolutely not! I was beating myself up all the way there.

We also have many people in our lives to forgive. For me it included my parents, brother, grandparents, relatives, bullies, my ex-husband, and my attacker. Talk about a long list, I had to face it all. I couldn't do it without God. It was too big for me alone. But with God, all things are possible.

For my parents, brother, grandparents, and relatives, it was a bit easier. They were family and I knew they loved me even though they had a hard time showing it. My ex-husband, the bully in school, and my attacker were another matter.

Forgiveness Journal

I knew it was going to be a journey when I went to forgive certain people. I created my forgiveness journal to help with the healing. I had to go through the pain to get to the other side. I know this isn't easy and it takes courage.

POWER IN FORGIVENESS

For my ex-husband, I had to detail out all the hurt. From the lies and manipulations, to the physical, mental, and emotional abuse. How he left me feeling through it all, and everything that came from every aspect of what I endured. It was brutal. I was exhausted and spent after doing this. But, I want to share the victory I found doing this. I was able to get past the emotion by naming them one by one. I was able to write the words I needed to heal from.

"I want to let you know that as of today, I am forgiving you from all that you have projected on me for many years. I am letting go of all the damaged emotions you caused me. If not for all the terrible things you put me through, I wouldn't be the strong and resilient person I am today. I am a leader in my church, and I am a confident, secure, and Godly woman. You can flee from my presence and I am no longer going to allow you to have power over me again. You can go!"

WOW! I felt the power return back to me, and it was precious and beautiful. I know I felt positive feelings when I became mature enough to assume the responsibility of what was going on in my heart. I can't forget all he did to me. But, I forgave him and found my control was back.

We all know of bullies in schools, no matter what age you are. Maybe you were one, you knew one or you were a victim of one. As you read in my Let It Go chapter, I had Jim. He was cruel in his ridicule of me, mocking me, and generally trying to steal my joy. I had to write out all the hurts and mean words that affected me. I went through the painful memories of what I felt from his words and actions. When I was done, I wrote and took back my sanity.

"Jim, I want to let you know, I am forgiving you and taking my power back. I forgive all the words you spoke and your actions. I choose to forgive you and let go of the past. You no longer control me or my future. Now you can go!"

I didn't need a lot of words to let go. It was all out at that point. I said what I needed to and I let it go. It was freedom from the past. If you have bullies in your life, you know it is hard to forgive them. We see that on the news with children who are tortured by bullies commit suicide or go on shooting sprees. How much more do we need to see to know what not letting go looks like. Take back control and reduce the power of the bullies by forgiving. Live a great and happy life. Do not let the bullies steal your joy. They have done that long enough.

How about my attacker? Some may have doubts about for-giving someone like that. But, the Bible does not distinguish sin from any other sin. It says to "forgive one another" not just the easier ones. And this was not easy. He was someone who stole my security from me. He hurt me physically, mentally, and emotionally. I had to spell it out and get out every scary moment. All the emotions that go with rape kits, doctor visits, police procedures, and line ups. All that trauma had to come out, because it was eating me alive. Once I did, I was able to let go and regain my place in the knowledge of who I am in Christ.

POWER IN FORGIVENESS

"Today, I want to let you know that I am forgiving you for all the horrible things you put me through, and I am taking my power back. I am secure and safe. You have no hold on me anymore. You can go now. Flee from my presence and never return." Although this exercise took all day, it was well worth it. I was exhausted, but it was a different kind of exhaustion. It was like a ton of weight had been lifted off me, and the chains that were choking me, were finally gone. I was free.

Over time, I felt I was on my way to becoming a whole person again. In the following months, I began moving from living in a victim mentality, to a survivor mentality. It wasn't easy, but God and I talked every day and night about this until I found the real Terri.

I know I shared hardcore things with you. I hope you know it wasn't an overnight process. I worked hard throughout the process. I wanted my sanity back and that wasn't going to happen unless I acted on it. You may not have stories like mine, you may have worse! Whatever your story is, it is horrible because it happened to you. Whatever it is, get rid of it. It is all poison that comes from bitterness and resentment. Get washed in the clean waters of God's word and forgive to stay clean.

I am a thriver in every sense of the word. I do not allow people or circumstances to derail me for very long. Remember, it is not about how many times you fall down, but how many times you get back up. Are you ready to get back up? I think you are. Don't let Satan keep you down. Take back control.

Your Beautiful Adventure Begins Here

Ephesians 4:32 says, "Be kind and tender to one another. Forgive each other, just as God forgave you because of what Christ has done."

Let's talk about the healing power of forgiveness. This is where the Holy Spirit tunes in beautifully to help you get there. Forgiveness is an incredible healing path for releasing those who you believe to have wronged you, not for their sake, but for yours. You can learn to forgive without any need to excuse or condone what has been done to you, and move beyond emotional wounds, rising and healing above the past. Through forgiveness, you can reclaim your power and strength, living life to the fullest.

Without forgiveness, we can remain locked in the past, giving our attention and energy to past conflicts, and experience the negative emotions. We don't have time for this much anger, fear, resentment, and shame. I know my life is packed full every day. I have my quiet time with God 1st, then I have clients to meet, a husband to take care of and dogs to walk.

When we forgive, we are making a choice. It is totally yours to make. It is a decision to let go of the past and that is where your beautiful adventure begins. You will reclaim your life and energy. I have experienced this first hand. I have used the techniques I have my clients use to reach that glorious moment. I have a long laundry list of people I had to forgive, as you well know reading my story. It is freedom in this. I do not let my past rule my future.

I looked at forgiving people as the hardest thing to do. It seemed unfair to me that they receive forgiveness. But, I cannot hold back forgiveness, not after what my God has done for me. I realized that it releases God to do His work in me as well as that other person. I couldn't have the energy to meet with others, be involved in my church, and lead groups. I have benefits that I never had while I was busy with revenge.

Ephesians 4:26-27 does not mince words when it says, "When you are angry, do not sin. Do not let the sun go down on your anger. Do not give the devil a foothold." Remember, the Devil must have a foothold before he has a stronghold. Do not make it easy for him. Fight by being quick to forgive.

Forgiving

I have had people hurt me so many times, and very deeply at that. I cried out to God day and night to make this hurt go away. I read in Colossians 3:12-13, "You are God's chosen people. You are holy and dearly loved. So, put on tender mercy and kindness as if they were your clothes. Don't be proud. Be gentle and patient. Put up with each other. Forgive the things you are holding against one another. Forgive, just as the Lord forgave you." So, I followed this command and I worked through it. It is almost always a process, rather than an isolated occurrence. It took time, but I did it.

One of the beginning steps I have my clients do is own up to their feelings. It involves taming your inner child who has caused a lot of havoc over the years, while dictating your life. Even as adults we can still throw tantrums when we don't get our way or become upset. We might manipulate others, seek revenge, or hurt other's feelings by accident. This inner child needs to be tamed.

We know when we have hurts like abortions, miscarriages, fired from a job, spouse issues, parents, or pets passing away, and the list can go on. We can get angry at our parents or even God. It is so easy to fall into this unforgiving state of mind. I know I have been mad at God at times. But, He wants us to be transparent and surrender to Him all those emotions so He can get to the root of it.

Forgive God for things not being the way you thought it would be. He knows what is best. He sees all ends. He knows your past, present, and future. So, trust Him even in the hard and tight spots. God is God and we are not. In Numbers 15:41 it says, "I am the Lord your God. I brought you out of Egypt to be your God. I am the Lord your God." Keep that in mind when you go to Him. God is just.

I highly recommend putting a circle around those I named and asking the Holy Spirit to bring up the junk so you can begin the forgiving process. Avoid blanket statements such as; I forgive my father, mother, brother or former spouse. You have to forgive specifically. For example: If your parents passed away you would say,

"Mom and Dad, I forgive you both for dying and leaving me orphaned. I understand the circle of life and I realize it happens. I am so happy for the time I had." I had to do this when my parents died. I was angry at both of my parents and God for their deaths. But that is the inner child in me.

Processing

My acceptance was letting go of the power struggle against what happened with my parents, family, ex-husband and loss. These were all things I couldn't change. I stopped playing the situation over and over in my head.

I dealt with the hurt by grieving to let it out to reduce the pain of the situation. Letting that strong emotional charge go lets you heal and keep the good memories. It is a process through the pain to find relief.

I was determined to no longer dwell on the hurts of the past. I rebuke them and say out loud, "I close the door on those old hurts once and for all!" And I choose to STOP thinking of it.

I tell myself daily and as needed, "I willingly and lovingly release and let go of all the people and circumstances that no longer serve me in a positive, powerful, and productive manner. When things come up I go to this immediately. I don't wait until I am past the point of no return.

Dream Big

You may be dreaming big dreams or having visions to do something great. When you forgive you have the energy and time to devote to it. The past doesn't have a chance to drain you. You can build your life around your dream instead of your hurts. This is what the goal is of our lives.

God dreamed big when He sent His son to die for us on the cross. Our pain and afflictions do not even come close to what He suffered. The humiliation, agony, hate being heaped upon Him. We know He knows, when that happens to us, He is aware of our suffering. Not too many people have had nails pounded into our flesh or a crown of thorns jammed on our heads. He has. We know He knows pain from all afflictions. He still forgave those hurting Him. Let us do the same to those that have hurt us. Pray for our enemies and forgive all.

Am I Forgiven?

People operate very much according to their feelings. They are the foundation of what we believe to be true. If we feel that someone likes us or rejects us, we accept that as truth. If we don't feel forgiven, clean and new, then we do not believe we are forgiven. I believe that is a dangerous road. I tell my clients that feelings are the most undependable part of us. They can derail us and make our lives a constant roller coaster ride. Until we have the emotions under control, they will rule us and allow us to fall.

If we still feel guilty after confessing to God, we can examine whether we have confessed to God the root of that sin. This is when listening to our feelings is helpful. They are like the weeds in our gardens and flower beds. They live and choke our plants until we see them and yank them out. God does the same thing with our feelings of jealousy, anger, bitterness, revenge, or hatred.

Guilt could be about making amends to those we offended. God may give us feelings of guilt that persist to accomplish that goal. If there is something in your heart you cannot shake, I bet odds it is guilt. I know I used to feel like I was constantly asking people to forgive me. So, I listed them out and asked God to reveal an unconfessed motive of which I had been unaware. When He reveals them, claim His forgiveness and move on. When you hold onto it, it can separate you from finding true intimacy with God. You may dance all around the issue, but the truth is, sin will build a wall between you and God. It will build even taller if you are not willing to forgive the people who have hurt you in the past or present.

Dr. James Dobson addresses this issue in his booklet on guilt saying, "A person with a tender conscience is often vulnerable to a particular kind of Satanic influence." And in 2 Corinthians 11:14, it tells us that Satan presents himself as an "angle of light." What better tool for spiritual discouragement could there be than feelings of guilt that cannot be forgiven. Finding what the truth is can be groundbreaking. But, Satan is always there trying to pull you away from the truth that you are forgiven.

What controls us most? Facts or feelings? What do you think you will discover as you fact-find your emotions? I pray you take the challenge and find what the truth of guilt is for you and put it to rest.

If I had ignored the opportunity to find my true self, I would have missed out on a beautiful life with God, myself, and others. I would have never been able to understand what forgiveness is all about when I forgave myself and others. I didn't give the Devil a foothold in my life, so I am here today, free and happy in my choices to be a forgiving Woman of God.

POWER IN FORGIVENESS

Tips from Terri

- Forgiveness can bring inner peace.

- Forgiveness can bring us new beginnings.

- Forgiveness can free us to become all we were created to be.

- Forgiving someone is a command from God.

- Write in your journal all those you need to forgive. Go after it from my examples.

Forgiveness is hard but well worth the effort.

I BELIEVE IN YOU!

CHAPTER SIX
The Crazy Prayer Warrior

What if I said this chapter could change your prayer life? Would you believe me? I love to pray specifically and watch God do His magic. You can ask my friends and family. This girl will pray the **craziest, wildest, and serious prayers** you can imagine. Over my 28+ years as a Christian, I have watched God build my faith through believing in Him that He loves me enough to answer them.

Throughout this chapter, I am going to take you on a ride with me as God unfolds His beauty when we pray to Him. Not just pray, but really believe He will answer us.

At my church, I have a reputation as being a prayer warrior as people witnessed my prayers coming true. I am not any different than you are. I am special to God, just like you are. I am often asked for my formula as a prayer warrior with answered prayers. I would like to share that with all of you. I believe this chapter will turn your prayer life around. This will be inspiring.

Deeper with God

I believe, if everyone in this world would pray at least once a week, this world would be a better place. But, the truth is, this world needs daily prayers. Think of it like being on Santa's lap. You sit on his lap, your pulse racing as you think of all the things you want. You ramble on the list of everything your little heart desires. Santa tells you he will see what he can do and off you went totally believing that he would bring you everything on your list. This type of thinking is only good as we spend quality time in prayer with God. He wants us to be childlike, believing He can deliver.

We can feel powerless when disaster strikes. We read about murders, rapes, domestic violence, and drug addictions that lead to family destructions. I see it all the time about my beloved Indianapolis. It can be overwhelming when we hear of plane crashes, terrorist attacks, earthquakes, tornados, volcanoes, and hurricanes. But, having a heart like Jesus did, is the answer. He would always immediately pray to His Father in all situations. If we go to God, we can have a higher prayer life every day. Let's take our prayer life to the next level when a crisis comes into our horizon. Because, a crisis will come. The Bible says we will have troubles. But, Jesus said, "I have overcome the world." So, we need His mindset.

There are so many things that can cloud our prayer life. I know when I get really focused on spending quality time in prayer with God, distractions will come my way fast. Satan knows when we are getting ready to pray and he will do everything in his power to destroy that time with our Father. I know for me, when I am ready to pray, my cell phone will ring, or my husband will come home unexpectedly, needing my attention. The dogs will need to go outside and laundry staring at me. The list goes on and we can get side tracked from spending quality time with God.

Sometimes I will rush through my conversation with God with most of the time focused on my wants and concerns. This is not what Jesus did. He removed ALL distractions from Him and went to a quiet place to pray. When we follow His example, it will make our time much more important and deeper with God. Facebook, Twitter, LinkedIn, email, and other types of social media can wait.

At one point, I challenged myself to not get on social media or my phone until I at least said good morning to God. Then I check it and move on to my quiet time. So, this is key to enhancing our prayer life and brings us to a point of being bold in our prayers. Less distractions can lead to longer times with God.

It is like getting ready to do a Bible study with friends, but at the last minute, they don't call to let us know they won't be there. They are a no-show. Don't we feel let down? God feels that way with us as well. We can become dull to the word after a while. Let us be like David who was always after God's own heart. In Hebrews 4:12 it says, "For the word of God is living and active. Sharper than any double-edged sword, it penetrates even to dividing soul and spirit, joints and marrow; it judges the thoughts and attitudes of the heart."

Prayer 101

My big start as a prayer warrior, as well as praying specifically for things, had humble beginnings. I just started studying the Bible with my spiritual mom, Tresanay Cannon. We were eating lunch at McDonald's when she began to pray. She prayed for our food, me, my salvation, everyone, and everything under the sun. I remember thinking that my fries were getting cold. When she finally stopped, I said, "Wow! You really like to pray long prayers!" She smiled at me and said, "You will do this too someday." I thought there was no way, I am too shy. Her prayer life was an example to me and over the years, I saw it help so many others. And now, I do pray "long prayers" like Tresanay.

It started one night after studying the Bible with women at my church. They asked me if I was going home, because I had not turned over my life yet. I said I was going straight home and got in my car thinking I want to go home. I had everything inside of me telling me to go home. But, I did not as you may have guessed. I drove straight to my favorite bar. I also challenged God for the first time. You will hear what I am talking about.

As I drove, I prayed to God, "If this is what You want for my life, you have to make it clear because I can't see straight right now." As I sat outside the bar, in my car, I cried and told God I was putting Him to the test tonight. If He passes, He has me for the rest of my life.

So, I walk in and expect to be greeted by everyone, but no one said hi. I went back to the pool room and my friends only said hello. They used to say, "Hey Terri! Are we going to party tonight?" I was puzzled. So, I sat and ordered a drink at the bar. It was awful. I told Daryl, the bartender, that it tasted like gasoline! He took a sip and told me I was crazy. I ordered something different and the same reaction. After trying six different drinks I gave up.

I went back to the pool room to play some pool. At that time, I was the #1 female pool champion in Indiana. I would hustle on the side to make extra money. I was very good and knew it. However, this night when I went to break the balls, there were about five that went soaring off the table and into the crowd. I never missed on the breaks. My pool coach, Andy, was concerned there was something wrong with me.

I was so frustrated that I began to smoke again. I had stopped when I started to study the Bible, but that night I lost my willpower. When I lit that cigarette, the smoke went right into my face, making my eyes water and my make-up run. I excused myself and fixed my make-up. When I came back, it happened again. I went to the restroom and told God, "I was supposed to be testing You, not the other way around. Here is your final test. I am going back to the pool room and grab my drink with my friend. We are going to sit at the other side of the bar where there is nothing going on and no smoke because there are no people over there. If the smoke comes my direction and causes my eyes to water, then You win, and I will gladly turn my life over to You right now. I will go home to call Tresanay and let her know I want to move forward with my studies and be baptized."

My friend and I walked over to the table and started to talk. Wouldn't you know, the smoke was in my face in seconds, causing me all sorts of eye problems. I stood up and told my friend, "I have to go home now." He asked me if I was ill. I said, "I am fine. I am going to start a new life as a Christian." I said goodbye to everyone and that was the last time I saw them.

On the way home, I begged God to not let me get in an accident. I wasn't saved, so I feared for my life that night. As soon as I made it home, I called Tresanay and ramped up my studies.

I truly believe it is okay to put God to the test. Abraham pleaded for Sodom in Genesis 18. He challenged God six times throughout this chapter when he asked God, "May the Lord not be angry, but let me speak just once more. What if only ten can be found there?" He was asking for God to hold back His righteous anger against Sodom. God wants to see the seriousness of our hearts when we are praying to Him. He did as Abraham asked so boldly.

I asked for specific signs and I had answered prayers that night. It taught me that we have power in our prayers, even when we challenge God.

Patience Is a Virtue

How many times do we pray for big things to happen in our lives and expect God to answer them right then? Will He answer our prayers immediately or in short order? It is His timetable, so let us keep a place of humility in our hearts. I know humility well, as God made me wait six long years to find a husband. I had to surrender to Him first and stop being in control.

It was on April 30th, 1993 when I was 38 years old, I became serious about surrendering to God my desire to have a husband. I dated in the church, but it turned out that I liked the men more than they liked me or they liked me, more than I liked them. I had my feelings hurt more than once.

That day in April, I prayed such a long prayer for a companion. I told God He would have trouble filling this tall order. I was very specific in my checklist for a husband:

- He has to be a Godly man that loves God completely.

- He has to be Kingdom focused.

- He has to love the lost.

- He would have to want to lead the singles after we marry.

- He has to love children.

- He has to have green eyes and brown hair.

- He has to love animals, but not be a hunter.

- He has to have a servant's heart for God's people.
- He has to be a steady provider for his family.
- He has to be funny and adventurous.
- He has to be a strong leader.
- He has to be compatible with me.
- He has to be 5'7" to 5'9" tall.
- He has to be 30-35 years old.
- He has to love nature and water.
- Last but not least, he has to have a bad back.

Now you may wonder why the last one was even on there. I needed someone who would be compassionate when I am slowing down due to my own weak back from a few accidents. It would not be a good fit for me to have a husband that wanted to climb Mt. Everest! So, I ended my prayer asking God to send him soon.

I headed down to Louisville, KY to stay at my girlfriend's home who was getting married. I was going to get fitted for my bridesmaid dress the next day. While we were eating the phone rang and it was for me. I was wondering who would be calling me down there. That was my first conversation with Scott Moore. He was from the Chicago church and was looking for leaders in the Midwest who led the thirty-something singles group. He was surprised I was a woman with a name like Terri.

THE CRAZY PRAYER WARRIOR

I further surprised him when I told him I was the founder of the group and it originated in Indianapolis. Then I asked what I could do for him. He said they were hosting a conference in October and he was reaching out to the leaders of the thirty-something singles. We spent forty-five minutes on the phone talking about everything. I started to become vulnerable with him and told him a little about my past. I had not done that so quickly before due to my past damaged emotions. But, there was something there.

When our conversation was drawing to a close, he asked me what I was doing in Louisville. I told him about the upcoming wedding and going to a Kentucky Derby party to play volleyball. I said, "I could only play a few games because of my accidents leaving me with a bad back." He said, "Wow! We are going to Lake Shore to play volleyball tomorrow, but I can only play a couple of games because I recently had a back injury."

I immediately told him it was nice to talk to him, but I had to go. He asked if I would come to Chicago and share with his committee how we launched the group for the singles. I said I would but, "I have to go."

I hung up the phone and my friend said, "Terri, you look like you have seen a ghost." I said, "Oh, my gosh, I think I just talked to my future husband!" She laughed saying, "Here we go again." Three weeks later, Tony, who lead the group with me, drove us up to Chicago. I was so nervous, but we prayed and asked God to move in our group. I had no idea what Scott Moore looked like, so I was focused on finding him.

He found me and escorted me to the podium to speak. At that time, I was not the speaker I am today. I was clinging to the podium for dear life, but I made it through and we all went to dinner. I still wasn't totally sure he was the man of my dreams or not, and I was so nervous, I don't remember any part of what we said at dinner.

Scott asked me to help head up the housing committee for the upcoming conference in May, so that led us to talking once a week. During one of our talks he asked me out on a date after the main session was over. I was delighted to go.

The day came for the conference and I had high hopes God would make it clear one way or the other. I was still having a hard time allowing God to be in control, so I was still a little unconvinced. I was looking around for him and found out he was in charge of several roles at the conference. We finally locked eyes! But that was it. He made no move to come over to see me. I was thinking to myself, "Dude, I just drove three hours to get here and you can't come over to say hi to me?" So that was strike one against him. I was not giving him much grace.

When it was time to leave for our "date" at 11:00pm, I thought we were going on a double date, but it ended up being about 20 people. Scott felt he had to be the leader, so I was in the back of the pack with my friends that I dragged along with me. The entire evening, he didn't say one word to me, not one single word. On top of all this, we had to sit in the hotel lobby eating cold pizza. So, it was strike two and three. In my mind, he was out and I was questioning God.

I walked back to my room wondering what just happened. My friends asked me what happened, and I said I didn't want to see him again and was disappointed the way it turned out. Unfortunately, we still had to work together on the conference. I saw him the next morning and put distance between us. He didn't even apologize for the night before and that ticked me off. I went to my classes for the day and we didn't see each other the entire day.

That night at the dance, I had a date with a guy from our Cincinnati church. I had my eye on several guys, but asked God to pick for me. Mark and I had a great time talking, dancing, and eating together. I couldn't get Scott off my mind though. I went to the restroom and thought about it all. I wasn't sure what to do. I had forgotten, through all of this that my girlfriends and I from Indianapolis were staying at his house while he was at a friend's. My heart sank to my stomach.

While I was in the restroom I told God that if Scott was the one he would apologize to me for our date being messed up, and God would give me at least a half hour to spend time with just Scott and I alone. I asked God for these specific things so I could see Scott without the responsibility he had been carrying. Scott had not been a Christian very long and this was his first conference.

When I left the restroom, I literally ran into Scott. We were face to face finally. He said he was sorry for the way the weekend turned out and he had been looking forward to spending time with me. I was feeling like God was working on my behalf. He heard my specific prayers and started to answer them.

After the dance was over, he helped us with our suitcases, but he asked me to ride with him to his house since my friend's car was pretty packed. I agreed and off we went. Within minutes he was back to himself. We talked about the conference, what we learned, and how to implement it all. It felt good, but part of me had my guard up and I was observing every move he made.

When I arrived at Scott's house, my friend's and I found roses for each one of us on the table and a note that said to help ourselves to anything in the house. He had an ironing board out with the iron and chocolate candies on our pillows. His house was immaculate, which was surprising for a man! He even had the refrigerator filled for us. One of my friends said, "If you don't want him, I will take him!" His kindness was really beginning to hit my heart. Then I found a note saying he would be there at 9:00am to make us breakfast and take us to church. My heart was beginning to melt. He did as he said, and all was fine.

We stayed in touch for the committee. The thirty-something singles in Indianapolis was hosting a Hollywood Blues night, so I asked him to be the leader for the Chicago church and he happily agreed.

Our conference approached and I was the master of ceremonies. It was set up like the Oscars and I was changing my outfits throughout the night. I was so looking forward to seeing Scott.

THE CRAZY PRAYER WARRIOR

In my dressing room I prayed a very specific prayer to God that went like this: "God, if Scott is the right one for me, then I ask you for specific things. When he walks in the door and sees me in my beautiful purple evening gown, please let him stop right in his tracks and say, 'WOW! You look beautiful tonight!' Also, please allow him to ask me to dance." God answered both prayers. He said exactly what I asked him to say and we danced! That night I could hardly sleep knowing God was moving in answering my prayers. I could hardly wait to see him the next day.

The next day, after the service, we went to a cookout and everyone was getting ready to play volleyball. Scott called me out to be on his team. I was so excited that I ran too fast and stepped in a hole in our backyard. I tried to push through the pain to impress him. It became too much though and I had to excuse myself. He noticed I was missing and found me. I told him what happened, and he wanted to take me to the emergency room. I fought it at first, but gave in. I had a broken ankle and now on crutches. He stayed overnight at one of my male friend's house. He came over the next day to say goodbye. I was happy and miserable all at the same time.

The rest is history. Scott and I were married September 24, 1994. God sent who and what I needed. I was bold in my prayers and very specific. God heard it and delivered.

I was like the persistent widow in Luke 18. She was adamant to the judge to give her justice against her adversary. He finally relented from her persistence. I believe I wore God out by asking Him two to three times per day for six long years, "When are you going to give me another husband when I am faithful to You, and I am 38 years old for goodness sake!" But, all this taught deep lessons in trusting God and learning to be patient as well as persistent.

Praying for the Sick

If you have a loved one or dear friend who is ill, do you up your prayer life? What do you do? Who do you turn to? Who do you trust to take care of them? Many times, do we trust only ourselves and not God? We leave Him out of the picture. In James 5:14-15 it says, "Is anyone among you sick? Then he must call for the elders of the church and they are to pray over him, anointing him with oil in the name of the Lord; and the prayer offered in faith will restore the one who is sick, and the Lord will raise him up, and if he has committed sins, they will be forgiven him." Since the Bible is our guide to living life to the fullest, we should follow this command.

In Jeremiah 29:11 it says, "For I know the plans I have for you,' declares the Lord, 'plans to prosper you and not to harm you, plans to give you hope and a future." It boldly states in this scripture that God will not harm us. I know what this means first hand.

In May of 2014, my husband had a mini stroke. He was rushed to the hospital with slurred speech, dizzy, and could not write his name well. He was diagnosed with a rare condition called Chiari Malformation in the brain. It is a condition where the neck and skull meet. The fluid cannot flow freely. They would have to push his brain up into his skull because it was dropping down into his spinal area. Then they would put mesh in place to keep the brain from going back down into that area. You want to talk about fully taking in James 5!

It was a frustrating search looking for a neurosurgeon under our insurance. When we found one, the Chiari condition was worse. Then came the three options from the doctor. He could get better, worse, or die. No wife wants to hear these words. She gave us a few minutes to absorb the news. The door shut and we just stared at each other for a few minutes in silence. Then we began to pray and ask for clear guidance from God on which way to proceed. Some patients lived without the surgery, but the pain gradually increased. That was no life. So, we told her we were going ahead with the surgery. It was scheduled for three months from that time. It was a trying three months. We were told to get our affairs in order and make arrangements, just in case.

When we arrived home, I went off to my private place by the lake to pray. I was trying to be strong for my husband, but I felt like the little girl inside was coming out full throttle, and I was afraid I would lose my Scott. I struggled for a week because I did not want to face this reality. As the time drew near, the pressure was on to get the will and funeral arrangements ready. I wanted to run away from all of this. But, as I got the little girl inside under control, I put the mature Terri in control and prepared for the worse, praying for the best.

To say I was praying my heart out was an understatement. Prior to the weeks before surgery, there were many things my husband wanted to get done to allow him peace of mind. Many projects around the house had to be neglected due to his busy schedule. It was breaking my heart to watch him get things accomplished, knowing what was ahead of him. He was going to be off work four to six months and that put a ton of pressure on me. But, Scott would always say, "God's got this!" Although this took me some time to digest everything happening around us, in my heart I knew I had no choice but to trust deeply in God more than ever. I prayed morning, noon, and night, believing God would come through for us.

It was three weeks before the surgery and my wonderful church said they would help support us while Scott was down. I was so deeply touched I cried and with tears in my eyes, I told God, "Thank you, Daddy!" Food was going to be delivered while he was recouping, and people would be visiting. What a blessing that was and so needed and welcomed.

I was still working at Beacon of Hope but had to take three weeks off to take care of Scott as much as possible. It was tough to be available for others, even though I was gone taking care of Scott.

June 15th, 2015 came fast. We had many friends from church and throughout the world praying for him, the doctors, nurses, and the hospital. Scott was cool and collected. God did have this. He said it and I know he believed it. I was very proud of my husband for his faith in trusting God. Since he was so calm, they would not give him a happy pill so I could not record him.

When the nurse came to take him to surgery, my heart was racing. I said a quick prayer to pull myself together for his sake. As I walked alongside of him, he reassured me saying, "God's got this." As the nurse allowed me another minute with him, we stared at each other. I said, "I will see you on the other side and I don't mean Heaven!" I promised on our wedding day I would make him laugh every day I could. This was no exception. But as the surgery door closed, I wondered if I would see him alive again. A nurse came by and asked if I was okay. I looked at her and said, "Oh my gosh! Now I understand what it means to give up complete control and totally trust God." I had absolutely no say, whatsoever, in my husband's outcome. If God wanted him that day, there was nothing I could do about it. I told Jesus to take the wheel and went to the waiting room where fifteen people were waiting to serve me and my family.

Scott's surgery lasted six hours. I was thinking back about the times he wanted to back out of the surgery. I would encourage him to stay the course. Thankfully he did. When the doctor was talking to us after the surgery, they said it was a good thing he got this done when he did because, had he waited any longer, he could have died. The fluid was barely flowing around the brain. Had it stopped, he would have died. I rose off my chair and thanked the doctors and thanked my God.

Scott recouped nicely for three months. He doesn't sit still long. Within two weeks he was able to attend church. This built the faith of the congregation greatly. On his year anniversary of his surgery I took him to Wolf Park in Lafayette, Indiana. We had reason to celebrate indeed.

Visionary Prayers

I am not only a crazy prayer warrior; I am also a visionary. I have stunned my co-workers and people at church with them. I have learned to ask God to make them abundantly clear. So buckle up as I take you through a visionary prayer and desire that God not only filled, but exceeded my expectations.

Casting Crowns is my favorite Christian band. In August of 2013, I had an idea to see if Beacon of Hope could get Casting Crowns in for a fundraiser concert. It was way out of our price range, so I had to put this on the back burner. People had doubts, but I stayed faithful and patient.

In January of 2014, they came to Indianapolis for a free concert. I received an email from the local Christian radio station who partnered with Beacon of Hope and was invited to be her guest to meet the band personally. Mark Hall, a youth minister in Atlanta, Georgia, wanted to share some preaching with the youth leaders in our community. Beacon of Hope has a Teen Talk Education

Program, so I was invited and on cloud nine. I had a list that I wanted God to fill.

- I find the location and I am early – Answered

- I get to meet and talk with each band member individually– Answered

- I get a picture taken with the band – Answered

- I get everyone's autograph – Answered

- I make a good impression on them for when I contact their agent for them to come to Indiana again for Beacon of Hope – Answered

- We develop a lasting connection – Answered

The concert was at 6:30pm but we got there at 4:00pm. My husband was in a boot cast and the ushers saw us and motioned us to go first. We had our choice of seats, so we were up front and center. This was a kiss from God.

When they stepped out on stage they saw me and waved. I wasn't sure if it was for me or not, but it was! My husband commented on my making an impression on them for sure. I said, "Thank you, Daddy, for this great day and night!" The door prizes came, and Scott won a T-shirt and Casting Crowns CD, *Thrive*. What a day.

February of 2014 rolled around, I was sitting at my desk and God started to nudge me to write an email to

Casting Crowns. I was thinking, "You want me to do what? Are you crazy? What am I supposed to say?" I ignored this crazy request and continued on in my day. But, God kept at me and I told him, "If you want me to write an email to Casting Crowns, then you will have to tell me what you want me to say."

I explained to the band manager who I was and what Beacon of Hope was about. I told them their songs meant a lot to me and helped me through rough times. I asked them to do a fundraiser with us when they come to Indianapolis. I didn't ask for a free concert, but if God moved their hearts to do so, then we would be happy with that as well. I shared I was a visionary and God was calling on me to act on His vision for this. I explained the proceeds would go to the Teen Talk program. I sent the email and said a prayer.

March of 2014, I was holding a staff meeting. In the middle of the meeting, I looked at the picture in the room with the word VISION and I froze. They thought something was wrong. I said, "Oh my goodness. I just had a vision we will be partnering with Casting Crowns for a large fundraiser at the Pepsi Coliseum in October for Domestic Violence Awareness Month. And you will all get to meet them." We all sat still, trying to digest it all. Finally, one of my staff said, "Terri, you are a visionary leader, so AMEN!"

Later that day as I was driving, I heard over the radio, "Hey, Casting Crowns fans. Did you hear they are coming to the Pepsi Coliseum on October 11th!" I had to pull over. I was shocked. I checked their website and sure enough they were coming. I prayed immediately for God to work on this. I wasn't sure how it would go since Melanie, their band manager, didn't answer my email. I wasn't sure if she even read it, but she had.

May of 2014, I was sitting at my desk when my office manager comes in and said there was a man on the phone who wouldn't give his name but wanted to talk to me. He was the owner of a production company. He said, "Terri, I had dinner with your favorite band the other night and your name and organization came up." I stopped him short and said, "Hey, hold the phone. How do I know you are not trying to sell me something? Who is my favorite band?" He told me Casting Crowns. I was at full attention to what he had to say.

He said one of the band members saved my brochure that I had given him in January. As they were praying for a non-profit to give back to, our name was brought up. You can imagine my shock. I literally fell off my chair and unable to speak for a moment. He also mentioned I would be on stage for at least five minutes to share about Beacon of Hope in front of 4000-5000 people. Also, for each ticket Beacon of Hope sold, they would give us $5.00 for our center.

I was frozen in my seat after we hung up. God had orchestrated this entire gift. My staff didn't know if I was for real or not. But, when it all sunk in, they were screaming, dancing, and praising God.

My prayer list for that concert was this:

- No snow, ice, rain, or hail – Answered

- For friends and family to meet the band – Answered

- My church family would buy 150-250 tickets – Answered at 250

- Beacon of Hope would raise $15,000 or more – Answered at $16,000

- For me not pass out on stage or forget my speech – Answered

In James 4 at the end of verse 2 it says, "You do not have because you do not ask." So, ask away and watch Him deliver.

Rain, Rain, Go Away

We have all planned outdoor events. Here in Indiana, we have all seasons and they can be ferocious. So, imagine my wedding day when the weatherman was calling for 60% chance of rain lasting the entire day. I was a little concerned because we planned to have our pictures taken outside. I asked my roommate, Amanda, to pray with me. I had waited six long years for a husband, so I was determined.

I woke up the next morning with excitement thinking God answered my prayers. But, instead of sunshine, it was pouring down rain. I immediately began to pray to God, begging Him to change it. I asked for blue skies and 70 degrees by 10:00am. God answered my prayers perfectly. It was a flawless and beautiful day.

As we went to Myrtle Beach for our honeymoon, we took a cab to our hotel. We told him we were here on our honeymoon and he said, "You picked the wrong week. We are supposed to have a hurricane with tornadoes, hail, and rain all week." My husband and I looked at each other and said, "That's what he thinks!"

The weatherman said the same thing the cabbie said. I told Scott, "You know what we need to do." So, we prayed immediately for God to change it. We asked for seven days of blue skies, 80-85 degrees and no adverse weather of any kind. And our good Father delivered. So much so that others were commenting on how wrong the weatherman was. We looked up to Heaven and thanked our God.

Examples for Us

All we have to do is look to the Bible for examples of answered prayers. Some crazy and wild. Some that were desperate.

In Genesis 24, the servant prayed for a wife for Isaac and did he not end up with Rebekah? He was specific in his prayers when he said in Genesis 24:43-44, "May it be that when I say to a young woman, 'Please let down your jar that I may have a drink too.' Let her be the one you have chosen for your servant, Isaac. By this I will know you have shown kindness to my master." You know the rest of the story. God answered his specific prayer with Rebekah.

In Hebrews 5:7 it says, "Jesus cried up to God with loud petitions and cries." His prayers got His Father's attention. He was not afraid to tell His Father all of His issues.

In Matthew 17, Jesus heals the demon possessed boy. He talks to the people and tells them if they have the faith of a mustard seeds they can move mountains.

In 2 Kings 5:6 it says, "And Elisha prayed, 'O Lord, open his eyes so he may see.' Then the Lord opened the servant's eyes, and he looked and saw the hills full of horses and chariots of fire all around Elisha." Talk about immediate prayers being answered. This is how we can pray too.

I could go on and on with the many examples of faithful prayers from God's people. God is before my husband, family, and career. He blesses me in lavish answered prayers beyond even my own expectations.

Tips from Terri

- Allow God to control your life.

- Start praying specific prayers.

- Make Him REAL in your life.

- Study out prayer.

- Start your own prayer group or chain going.

- Give God all the details of your life (He knows them anyway)

CHAPTER SEVEN

God, Bless Me Indeed and Enlarge My Territory

One evening my husband said he wanted to speak to me about something that was troubling him. "Honey, I love you and believe in you, but I am concerned about your spirituality. Where did the person I fell in love with go? The woman who would lead any group in church or help anyone in need. Where did she go? You are becoming a hermit, never wanting to leave the house besides church and work. What is going on?" I looked at him like he was crazy.

As I looked back, I realized I was burned out in my life with all the demands on me. On top of being a wife, mother, church leader, working, and helping some of my friends with advice, I was going through "the change." I felt like the life was being sucked out of me. He, of course, saw how I was feeling and said, "We are going to pray right now for you to be yourself again and start being used by God, because you have many gifts and talents." Well, needless to say, I was stunned by all of this and, perhaps even mad at him. But, we prayed together and got through it.

Sometime later, I came across the book, *The Prayer of Jabez* by Bruce Wilkinson. In the book, the author's advice was to recite The Prayer of Jabez every day. I did this because it said it really worked. I don't know if I really believed it at the time. Two weeks went by and I didn't feel or see anything different. I stopped reading, but somehow, God put it back on me to keep reading, so I obeyed.

In 2007, I was doing a fundraiser for Home and Garden Party. I was the Fundraiser Coordinator and we were raising funds for a domestic violence children's program. We had 4 people plus the shelter's pastor. Normally, we would have 50-60 at these events so this was a bit off. But, as usual, God has a plan. The pastor informed us there is a need for another domestic violence organization on our side of town. He said, "Terri, I just met you tonight, but I think God is calling you to lead this. All of you ladies." I was speechless. I told him I always wanted to open a pet shelter. All four ladies that night were domestic violence survivors, including myself. So, for two weeks after, all of us were having a hard time sleeping at night after hearing about domestic violence statistics. I invited the women over to my house to pray about it. To make a long story short, God called us to open Beacon of Hope in 2009 to serve women, men, children, and pets of domestic violence.

I had to start a board of directors, having no experience in this, and I was voted president. I then became the executive director and remained so until 2016, when I left to start Terri L Moore & Team.

GOD, BLESS ME INDEED AND ENLARGE MY TERRITORY

There is no question in my mind that God moved in mysterious ways to enlarge my territory, giving me a community to lead. This is the God we serve, go big or go home.

In 2015, my executive coach pulled me into her office to discuss something. Shamara brought me to her big white board and wrote out things that left me speechless. She wrote that she saw me as a speaker, empowerment coach, workshop leader, radio talk show host, and author. She told me that my time at Beacon of Hope was coming to an end, and a new chapter was beginning. Taking me further than I dreamed while enlarging my territory in ways I never saw coming.

Praise be to God, I am doing everything she said I would do, and I am having the time of my life. I will be doing this as long as I have to live. God was faithful in His words to me from Jeremiah 29:11, telling me He had plans to prosper me with hope and a future. Enlarging my territory was beyond anything I had experienced before.

The Prayer

Jabez was more honorable than his brothers. His mother had named him Jabez, saying, "I gave birth to him in pain." Jabez cried out to the God of Israel, saying, "Oh that you would bless me indeed and enlarge my territory! Let your hand be with me, and keep me from the evil one." And God granted his request.

-1 Chronicles 4:9-10

The Prayer of Jabez is not magic and it is not selfish. It is a prayer that is an expression of your heart to God's. Let's take a look into the heart attitude of Jabez by looking at 5 distinctives in the word of the prayer.

First, this prayer is very personal and intimate. Jabez did not ask for God to bless the world. He said, "Please bless me." Praying for the world is a great thing to do, but we should not forget ourselves. We come to God in prayer empty so that He fills us back up to serve His people. Just like cars, we run and run, but we still need fuel. That is what happens when we go to God and ask Him to bless us. It is more than okay to pray this way.

God has blessings to hand out to His children daily. Matthew 21:22 says, "You can pray for anything, and if you have faith, you will receive it." This makes me stop and ask myself, "I wonder how many blessings I have not received because I have not asked or believed I would get."

Secondly, the prayer is not specific. If we limit our expectations and request to one specific way we want God to bless us, we may be limiting ourselves. That is not the intent of The Prayer of Jabez. God's blessing is,

GOD, BLESS ME INDEED AND ENLARGE MY TERRITORY

by definition, directed and determined by God alone. Not man. We may be praying a valid prayer, but allow for specific to be about your situation, not how its answered. Ultimately, there is only One who knows the most appropriate and fulfilling blessing for you. That is God. Trust Him to answer your prayer most effectively.

Thirdly, the prayer does not ask for small provisions, but for abundant blessing. When we ask for large blessings, He will wisely know how and when to answer. He is not stingy with anything He has for us. He loves enthusiastic prayer and wants our passion, which expresses great transparency and fervor, which God welcomes.

Fourth, the prayer is not time specific. This allows God to bless us even greater whenever, wherever, and however He wants. Praying for God to bless me by next Friday or Monday is not at the heart of The Prayer of Jabez. He never gives God a timeline and yet it says that God granted his request. So, follow that logic in your prayers.

Finally, this is not a weak wish. When you go to sporting events, you don't see people sitting in the stands like statues. They are cheering wildly and praying to God that their team wins. Scott and the dogs do not like to be in the room with me when the Indianapolis Colts football team is on. I love this team, so I get a little carried away. But, we can do this too with our prayers. Let us get our adrenaline pumping, our hearts racing, cheering God on so much that we lose our voices for a few minutes. Get that excitement for our prayer life to God.

When you pray as Jabez did, you are asking with everything inside of you being mobilized into a relationship with God. It is not just reciting a prayer. It is walking into the heart of the prayer of faith as Jabez did.

The Smallest Scripture but Mighty

The prayer itself is very tiny but packed with a valuable testimony of the understanding and loyalty that Jabez had to God. Look at how Jabez asked God to enlarge his territory. He wanted more influence, responsibility, and opportunities to be used for God's purposes. Be ready when you pray this prayer. I have been praying this prayer for nine years and I may have to stop to get caught up with the enlarged territory God has already given to me.

Exodus 14:14 says, "The Lord will fight for you. Just be still." Let us learn to be still and listen to His voice. I know I have trouble doing this when things surround me. But His word is truth, so let us do this. Pray 'The Prayer of Jabez' and be still, for God is fighting for you.

The Prayer for Blessing

Do you want God's blessings so much that you ask with hunger and urgency? The large and small blessings that surround us come from God. When you ask God to bless you a lot, you are inviting Him to engage in His favorite activities. After all, we are commanded in the Bible to ask God for everything. 1 Thessalonians 5:17 says, "Never stop praying."

Some of God's greatest blessings are reserved for those who ask for a truly abundant life. What blessings have you not asked God for because you were too afraid to ask, or you did not feel like it would really matter to God? But, we see in the Luke 18:1-8, the persistent widow kept asking. She wouldn't stop and she had nothing to give.

Jabez made a simple prayer, but it was asking God to bless him straight up. I asked God to bless me with a husband for six years! He finally did. Not on my time, but on His. So, keep that in mind as you pray so that you might faithfully, as well as successfully advance, and take new ground for God.

Let Your Hand Be with Me

Jabez was calling on God for protection, provision, and strength. He was confident and reliant in the power of God, and we see that in the way Jabez was calling on God to keep His hand on him. God's Hand implies power.

After reading this mighty scripture over the years, I came out with a new and deep conviction that the Hand of God is released when we dare to step boldly out of our comfort zone and serve Him.

The Hand of God is divine intervention. He breaks through into our world, in our time and space to perform His will in such a way that amazes us and causes people to say, "Look what my God just did!" It is time to start sharing with others what God is doing in your life. When we don't share God's blessings with others, we leave them out of our joy. Don't you just love to see people's faith rise when we share what God does in your life? I sure do. I see it all the time with people in my church, my clients, and my family and friends.

The Hand of God is not guided by our wishes or desires, but by His will. He can do anything He wants to for anyone. His will is wisest and best. God is good all the time. We know this by the movement of His Hand resulting in miracles. It may not be in the way we feel or in our circumstances. But, we know His Hand brings change.

He opened up His Hand by saving mine so many times. As you read the fingerprint of my time on this earth, I hope you see what I know. He stepped into my misery and made it my mission over and over again. It was a rough road, but I know that it has sharpened me to be used more by God for His magnificent purposes. I don't take credit for myself. I know who the Prayer of Jabez focuses on. God. But, I am His child and so are you. You have access to the Father to ask Him to have His Hand be with you.

Keep Me from Evil that I May Not Cause Pain

When Jabez prayed, "Keep me," he was asking God to act in protection. But, his motive for not wanting evil in his life was so profound when he said, "That I may not

GOD, BLESS ME INDEED AND ENLARGE MY TERRITORY

cause pain." When we participate in evil, we cause pain and grief to others as well as ourselves. But, even more so, our relationship with God suffers. Jabez wanted to protect his relationship with God, as well as having protection. He knew what was most important.

We see this played out in our lives. I have certainly been hurt by groups of people as well as singly. I did have evil thoughts in my heart during some of those times, but this prayer has helped me through it. We are human, so this can happen to any of us.

We know we are under attack every day as Christians, but we are still battle worthy. We have an enemy. He wants us back under his control and authority, using any circumstance to do so. He will plot and plan and use anyone he needs to that will distract us. He will cause friction with God, spouses, family, friends, and Godly people. We can get complacent as we mature in our faith. So the armor of God in Ephesians 6 is a serious matter.

When was the last time you cried out to God to send more protection and reinforcements into your situation? Many of God's people rise to the challenge to take the new territory and find themselves under attack, both spiritually and physically. This causes some to turn away from praying this prayer. I could have done that too, but inherently, I wanted to be loved and give love. Having evil thoughts and feelings would only destroy me. Jabez knew this for many reasons as we see in his bold prayer. He knew what could lead him far from God.

What It Means to Pray for Protection

Do you think it's wrong to ask God to minimize our suffering? It really isn't. God cares about the pain we experience and concerned for the condition of our relationship with Him. He knows that sin causes far more harm than physical pain or hardship.

The prayer for protection is not only for the future, but also for today. Praying about evil keeps you alert to the spiritual battle that rages around and within you. One of Satan's favorite tricks is to create a false sense of security so that we might drop our defenses.

Sometimes there is a misconception out there about God knowing when we are tempted, so prayer isn't necessary since He will protect us. The fact is, praying for protection will greatly affect the degree of whether or not you are tempted. So, keep vigil.

I know what evil can do. Evil stared me down in the face with my ex-husband who murdered someone in cold blood, and when I was sexually assaulted at the mall. I could have been dead in either circumstance. I wasn't even praying for His protection and He still gave it to me. What a good God I serve.

Not Just Geography

I have my dog, Lilly. She is a love that is beyond borders. I got her a little over a year after the passing of our last dog. I had grown up with a pet almost all my life. When my husband wanted to wait for a while longer, I

GOD, BLESS ME INDEED AND ENLARGE MY TERRITORY

prayed. I prayed specifically for this to change. Then came my birthday and he asked me what I wanted. I said a puppy and he said yes. I know this sounds like a simple story about getting a dog, but the fact is, enlarging our territory is about every facet of our lives. He wants all of our hopes and dreams no matter the size or what it looks like.

Perhaps we have our own ideas how things should work out in life, but God's ways are not our ways. In the Bible, Jacob wrestling with God in Genesis 32:22-32. In verse 26 Jacob told God, "I won't let you go unless you bless me." He was bold in his prayers and he was bold in his language with God. His territory was enlarged after that when he was blessed by God and his brother, Esau, forgave him and helped him. Mary had The Son of God without any man touching her. Talk about enlarging her territory! She was a woman who prayed for a family with all her heart. Look at what God blessed her with.

I see in my own life that I needed my territory expanded and it wasn't about geography. It was about my reaching the lost. The wounded and left behind. I saw the need for the victims of domestic violence and God expanded my territory meeting so many people and helping me to save as many lives as I could. And when I took the turn to Terri L Moore & Team, that was, and still is, uncharted territory for me. I still do not know what it will all look like over the next few years of my life. I plan on stepping out of the boat and walking on the water as often as I can. It takes me looking back at my blessings to do that. I see His Hand on my life and the blessings He sent are more than I have even asked for.

My territory was enlarged when I trusted God would bless me and I would be protected by Him and not by any man. I gave up so much of what I thought I wanted and needed, but what God gave me in return was bigger than my own dreams. He fostered that love inside of me even when I didn't know Him. My Prayer of Terri needed to reflect the Prayer of Jabez so that I could experience the growth that was waiting for me from Heaven.

Proverbs 3:5 says, "Trust in the Lord with all your heart. Do not lean on your own understanding." Ask for your dreams and trust the Lord your God to deliver in big ways. People who have, yield big results.

Are You Ready? Really Ready?

If you are really ready for God to enlarge your territory, you better fasten your seatbelts. 1 Chronicles 4:10 says if God doesn't put His hand upon you, it will all fall apart. We know that it is truth. We all have had moments when we have taken ourselves down the road to the point where we know our best efforts are doomed to failure unless He comes through. He wants us to invite Him into this. But, if we play things safely, we may never know this. Venturing beyond where we feel safe in our prayers is going to allow us to see God's hand working powerfully in our lives.

GOD, BLESS ME INDEED AND ENLARGE MY TERRITORY

What things in our lives may have been hindering us from venturing out of our comfort zones? It may be fear of failure, doubt, insecurity, or people telling us that we won't make it. When I was called by God to start Beacon of Hope and Terri L Moore & Team, I had all those feelings. I didn't want to get out of the boat of my comfort zone. I had to make the leap of faith of my lifetime. I tell my clients that I know what they are feeling because I have been there and am now on the other side.

I wasn't always ready to be a radio talk show host or speak in front of thousands. I didn't have a clue how to find the courage to write a book, but here I am. God is always enlarging my territory, but I had to let Him. I had to give Him full authority. He has shown me more of my strengths He made in me when I was still in His thoughts before time began. But, He knew when I was ready, and now I am on the road He set me on. It is a wild ride at times, and I can't believe what He has given me to do, but I see it unfold every day. Being ready means being ready to serve God in big ways and He will enlarge your territory so you can do more work for Him, as well as be successful in your life, and that can all lead to happiness.

Stepping out of our comfort zone can yield more power in our lives. Look around at the people who are successful in your church. Ask them what they do in their prayer life. You will see boldness in their prayers. They know what blessings God has in store as they see their lives unfold.

Tips from Terri

- I encourage you to pick up the book, *The Prayer of Jabez* by Bruce Wilkinson and read it.

- Write things down that may be hindering you from venturing out of your comfort zones.

- Start reciting *The Prayer of Jabez* every day for the rest of your life.

- Purchase a journal and begin to write down every blessing that comes your way.

- Review your blessings when you are confronted with hard times.

- Remember you are worthy to pray just like Jabez did.

CHAPTER EIGHT
Will the Real Me Please Stand up!

Hopefully by now you are well on your way to discovering the NEW YOU. Let me ask you a question that I ask my clients every single time. On a scale from 1 to 10, with 10 being the highest number, where do you see yourself loving that person staring back at you in the mirror? My friends, if you gave yourself a 5 or under, then I really need to speak to you one on one. Do you realize you are a gift from God? It really hurts Him when we do not score ourselves any higher than that.

Have you ever heard of the phrase, "The old is gone, the new is here?" This is how God would like to see us as His children since He wiped our slate clean when we entered into a relation-ship with him. Some of us still do not understand the depth of what He did for us on the cross.

Let's break it down. We were full of sin and He sent His one and only Son to die on the cross for us for two reasons. One, to wipe our slate clean from all the junk we contaminated our lives with. Secondly, to give us life to the fullest, not half full. However, in my coaching sessions with my clients, they keep beating themselves up with the old video tapes playing over and over in their heads that they are not enough. This is not true, we are enough. When we entered into our relationship with God, this was God telling us we are worthy to enter His kingdom. How wonderful is this? As I spent time listening to songs that have spoken to my spirit for years, I shed tears in reflection of the awesome experience of God stepping into my life and extracting out almost EVERYTHING that is not like Him. One of my favorite songs is from Casting Crowns, *The Voice of Truth,* because it speaks to that truth.

As I have shared in several of my chapters, well over twenty years ago I went on a journey to find the real person inside of Terri Lee Moore. Recently I reflected back and thought about all the people I hurt when they were saying nice things about me that I would not believe about myself. It really convicted me that I was rejecting those people with their kind words. You see, when we are buried under all types of damaged emotions, it is hard to understand who we truly are. We are constantly asking ourselves the question, who is the REAL me?

What does it mean to be authentic? Let's start with questions dealing with awareness. Who are you? Let's look in the awareness area. Who are you? What is your story? What is the degree of your self- awareness? Do you understand of why you are the way you are? Are you living in the past, present, or future? Do you have potential? Where are you stuck? What is your identity?

Do you understand your inner child? How about your emotional self? Are you moody? What are your fears? What does your inner filing system look like? How much blame, shame, and guilt are you carrying?

Let's talk about a big area that affects who we are. Did you know if you are not taking care of yourself you are expressing to God and others you do not value yourself? Are you a person who doesn't care about yourself enough to deal with bad habits and addictions? How are you dealing with stress and pain in your life? Are you ignoring it, thinking it will go away? How about negative feelings making an impact on your body? I know this because of my bad habits and addictions from my past. I did not care about making certain I was taking care of myself.

The final area is the intuitive self. Are you accepting yourself? Are you learning to thrive? Are you learning to love yourself? Re-remembering who I am before God, myself, and others? Are you loving life?

Your intuition will tell you intimate and important things nobody else will. And it will tell you things your own mind will argue with.

Let's Break It Down

Are you learning to love yourself? You are the only one who can answer this question. Please allow me to give you a little insight. How many times a day do you say negative things to yourself? Can you look in the mirror and love that person back? Loving yourself begins simply by understanding who created you. When I was learning to love myself, I would train myself to say five positive things a day that I liked about me. This one was a toughie for me because of my past. When I would catch myself saying negative things, I would snap my fingers three times. This would actually "snap" me out of my negative thinking. My friends, I want you to stop self-sabotaging yourself. You must learn to be kind to yourself and to accept yourself. I can promise you when you learn to accept yourself, you will begin to enjoy your life much more.

Finding Yourself in an Abundant Lifestyle
What does it mean to live an abundant lifestyle?

Living an abundant lifestyle should be a goal for everyone. It's what can truly establish happiness and ensure that you are on the right path in life. It tells you that you're prosperous. It helps you avoid pain, suffering, and general struggle. The Bible tells us that God will often test us in prosperity, and that prosperity is not always equal to abundance. There are plenty of people who are prosperous but who don't live in abundance. By contrast, there are many more people who live abundantly but, who are not necessarily prosperous. But, it's an abundant lifestyle that we should strive towards.

Abundance may not be what you think

The magazine, *Christianity Today,* featured a discussion of "prosperity vs abundance." It was recounting the stories in Hebrews 11 of the faithful believers who were imprisoned, tortured, mocked, scourged, and stoned…living lives devoid of both prosperity and abundance. Yet while they ultimately lost their freedom, wealth, families, and in some cases, even their lives, they were nevertheless, abundant in life because they had deep-rooted joy within them. They had everything they needed to have a happy and strong faith.

What else does the average person today need to live "abundantly?" I believe it means that you need harmony and balance in every area of your life. From philanthropy to physical rewards, to free time, and to having a spiritual connection.

It's not always about finances

There are plenty of people who have the life they want, yet they wouldn't be considered "rich" by the rest of society. The sooner you understand this, the easier it will be to live an abundant lifestyle and be truly happy.

Ask yourself if you are happy where you are

From time to time, are you happy where you're at? Are you happy at work? Happy at home? Happy at church? Happy in society? What about other areas of your life? If you're not currently happy in these areas, some changes are in order. Notice that the question didn't ask whether you are happy with your finances because it doesn't matter how much you're making. You can be happy making any amount of money, as long as you're happy in other areas of your life. Are you in a good marriage? Are you surrounded by people who love you? Do you enjoy going to work every day? If you aren't at peace with your decisions throughout life, this is where changes need to be made.

Next Steps to Transformation

What's needed to begin living abundantly? What do you need to do in order to make a transformation to the abundant lifestyle you want? It's not as easy as simply going out and buying something in order to make it all perfect. It requires a journey in order for you to transform your way of thinking, your activities, your community, your body, your health, your stamina, agility, peace of mind, and other manifestations of an abundant life.

Making a transformation requires that certain goals be set, pursued, and achieved.

Additionally, there are ways to fast track your goals through daily affirmations, and just this addition to your day can have a significant impact on your life. Write down all the goals you want to meet. This includes establishing smaller targets so you can hit your bigger goals without becoming frustrated in the process. You can live life in abundance, but it may take some time, plus, changes in the way you think.

Knowing Your Living an Abundant Life

It's easy to talk about an abundant lifestyle, but how do you know when you're truly living "the good life?" You may be happy, but there may be room for more happiness. Here are just five areas of the abundant lifestyle you can explore to determine whether you're living the life you want.

Philanthropic Activities – It is important to live a life of service and a life of helping others. What acts of service make your heart sing? There may be one activity that you're more passionate about than others. It might be helping the homeless, volunteering at the local shelter, or even building schools in third world countries. It doesn't matter what fires your imagination, but it does need to be something that makes you feel full even just thinking about these acts of service. By participating in philanthropic activities, you can begin to lead a rich and rewarding life.

Physical Rewards – The tangible rewards of your success can be your home, car, boat, and other possessions. But at the same time, remember that these are acknowledgments of all that you have achieved, but not a bandage to mask emotional pain that you're dealing with.

Additionally, be careful that you're not using physical rewards as a way of identifying who you are in the world. They should simply exist in your life to inspire you to push forward and achieve more.

Playtime – It's great to have a successful career, but this means nothing if you don't also have time to play with plenty of ways to disconnect from your daily responsibilities. Playtime can be a daily lunch in the park, the luxury of an extra-long workout, a three-day weekend at the beach, a two-week vacation, a lengthy sabbatical, going to your favorite restaurant, or something else that you enjoy. How you will play, and when, is a question you must continually ask yourself.

If you cannot answer that question, or if you cannot remember the last time you played, you're not in abundance within this area yet. And playtime needs to be a focus to help create harmony within your life and recharge your soul.

Spiritual – Spirituality is often believed to be religion, but it is not. It's simply an ongoing awareness of a greater spirit. For me that means God. For others, spirituality is the seeking of inner grace, peace of mind, gratitude, mindfulness, and simply being still. Without having this spiritual component to your life…with-out this unique connective and meditative time to yourself, it can be difficult to remain focused, positive, and happy.

Body – Finally, in order to live an abundant lifestyle, you have to love your reflection in the mirror. If you're not happy with your physical body, including appearance, weight, health, and more, it's time to create "a new you." Just pursuing the body, you want can be a journey that helps you achieve happiness and abundance. Whether this means losing weight, overcoming a bothersome condition, improving your nutrition, clearing up your skin, or anything else, the focus needs to be on you. Take a journey towards intentional good nutrition and exercise and see how it transforms your physical body, as well as your overall well-being. **If you do this, you will no longer be wondering, "Will the Real Me Please Stand Up."**

Life Hits You out of Nowhere

When life hits us out of nowhere, it can feel like we are barely hanging on. This is exactly what happened to me and my husband last year when we found out he had to have the serious brain surgery. This definitely tested our security in God each and every day.

Tests that Rock OurSecurity

Security Test #1

How about when life seems unpredictable and uncertain? When I said Happy New Year to 2016, I had no idea what was in store for me. I had no idea God would change my life and use me to serve many individuals in making peace with their past in order for them to find their vision and dreams. I also had no idea I would become an international author this year.

What kind of security test have you experienced? Perhaps your career is struggling, financial problems, marital problems, bad diagnosis of an illness. All of these listed can test our insecurities in God and ourselves. It can be a constant, hair raising, stomach turning flux.

The truth is, God uses change to change us. He doesn't use it to destroy us or to distract us, but to coax us to the next level of character, experience, compassion, and destiny.

When I am feeling all secure, and knowing I am God's best friend, a crisis comes into my life, and then the testing time begins. I can hear God saying, "I need to toughen you up for the next round." Are we going to trust Him as our rock and security, or are we going to throw in the towel and become insecure? We must hold onto God when life throws us curve balls. Who do you run to when your emotions are about to take you down? Do you run to your Heavenly Father? I can honestly say I blow it from time to time. I am asking God every day to enlarge my territory. I only want to become better and better for God.

When You Long to Be Healthy and Whole

Security Test #2

In 1 Corinthians 10:13, it states, "The temptations in our lives are no different from what others have experienced. And God is faithful. He will not allow the temptation to be more than we can stand. When you are tempted, He will show you a way out so that you can endure." By the grace and power of God, I've had the exhilarating joy of winning many battles, some of them tougher than others. However, insecurity is a tough area for all of us to overcome.

Especially with females, because this is deeply woven into the fabric of our female soul to deal with. We must learn to trust God and not let anything come our way to derail us.

Here is our challenge: To let the healthy, utterly whole, and completely secure part of us increasingly overtake our earthly selves until it drives out every emotion, reaction, and relationship.

When We Lack Confidence

Security Test #3

I truly believe God loves us so much that when we are lacking in confidence, He will place things in our lives to where we are either going to have to sink or swim.

In the last 9 years, I have seen my confidence level grow to the point I am humbled by God's love for me. I have learned to develop skills such as; public speaking, coaching, starting a non-profit organization from scratch, leading workshops, seminars, media promotion, social media skills, and learning how to write a book and much more. When I look back over the last nine years, I don't even recognize that person. To God be the Glory!

Moses is my favorite character in the Bible besides Jesus. Moses had insecurity problems just like you and me. Think about the time when God told Moses he was going to lead the Israelites. He gave Moses this long speech about how it was going to be done. And what was the next thing that came out of Moses mouth? "Please Lord, send someone else to do this. I have never been eloquent in tongue or speech." To me, this doesn't sound like Moses was secure with himself. However, he trusted God and he went on to do something great. The beauty of Moses wasn't his super humanity, but his unwillingness to let his weaknesses, feelings, and fears override his faith. Like us, the worst enemy he had to fight in the fulfillment of his destiny, was himself.

I am very proud of myself that I did not let my fear override my faith when God was calling me to open a domestic violence organization in 2007. And then to open Terri L. Moore & Team in July of 2015. Did I have fear, anxiety, worry, and doubt. Yes, I sure did, but with the help of God, I overcame it. Mandisa, a Christian artist, quotes this scripture from her album, *Overcomer*.

WILL THE REAL ME PLEASE STAND UP!

"You dear children, are from God, and have OVERCOME them, because the One who is in you is greater than the one who is in the world."

1 John 4:4

What Are You Lacking Confidence in Today?

Perhaps you are lacking confidence in financial problems, relationship problems, health problems, or the like. I am encouraging you, and myself, to begin to trust God more with all of these problems. The ones I mentioned are hard core problems and can certainly rock your world. But our God is stronger.

The many lessons I have learned through my life experiences is, the enemy of our soul will never have to worry about what kind of damage you could do to the Kingdom of God, if he can get you to buy the lie that you are incompetent, weak, stupid, fat, or ugly. This is a lie from Satan. This garbage is not from God. Please stop allowing Satan to get the best of you.

When You Are Searching for Significance and Value

Security Test #4

Security test four deal with Psalm 139: 1-18.

FACE TO FACE WITH GOD

You have searched me, LORD,
and you know me.
2 You know when I sit and when I rise;
you perceive my thoughts from afar.
3 You discern my going out and my lying
down; you are familiar with all my ways.
4Before a word is on my tongue
you, LORD, know it completely.
5 You hem me in behind and before,
and you lay your hand upon me.
6 Such knowledge is too wonderful for me,
too lofty for me to attain.
7 Where can I go from your Spirit?
Where can I flee from your presence?
8 If I go up to the heavens, you are there;
if I make my bed in the depths, you are there.
9 If I rise on the wings of the dawn,
.if I settle on the far side of the sea,
10 even there your hand will guide me,
your right hand will hold me fast.
11 If I say, "Surely the darkness will hide me
and the light become night around me,"
12 even the darkness will not be dark to you;
the night will shine like the day,
for darkness is as light to you.
13 For you created my inmost being;
you knit me together in my mother's womb.
14 I praise you because I am fearfully and wonderfully
made;
your works are wonderful,

WILL THE REAL ME PLEASE STAND UP!

I know that full well.
15 My frame was not hidden from you when I was made
in the secret place,
when I was woven together in the depths of the earth.
16 Your eyes saw my unformed body;
all the days ordained for me were written in your book
before one of them came to be.
17 How precious to me are your thoughts, [a] God! How
vast is the sum of them!
18 Were I to count them,
they would outnumber the grains of sand—
when I awake, I am still with you.

We are all desperate for significance. This very need is built into our human hard drive to send us on a search for God who can assign us more significance that we can handle. He not only notices us, but He never takes His eyes off of us. Now this statement sends chills up my spine.

We must remember humility is a crucial component in true security. It's the very thing that calms the beast of pride. We find our lives when we lose our pride to humility to something much larger.

My life goal is to continue to be a woman of valor and strength. I long to become more like the Proverbs 31 woman, where I can laugh at the days to come. I am not quite there.

To go from being an insecure person to a secure person it will take effort. Many affirmations about yourself must come your way on a daily basis. I am encouraging all my readers to take the positive chart on the last page of this chapter and begin to say these words out loud for seven days. Even if you do not feel these words, please say them anyway. You are retraining your brain and your heart to think you are. I am 100% confident you will become the majority of these on this list. When I was finding myself, I could only repeat two or three in a confident tone. Now, I can repeat all of these except for a couple in which I am still working on.

When we allow God's truth to eclipse every false positive and let our eyes spring open to the treasure we have, there in His glorious reflection, we will see the treasure we are. My friends, this is when you will see God ***Face to Face.***

We seek purpose when we are not in touch with who we really are. When you discover who you are, at the deepest place of your being, you will find yourself.

As I write this last chapter, tears are flowing down my face. I am very honored God chose me to be in His Kingdom and have the beautiful life I do. I am honored He called me to write this book. I am especially grateful to God. He was there for me when I was finding my REAL self. He will be there for you too.

I have thoroughly enjoyed our time together and I am sad it is coming to an end for now.

At Terri L. Moore & Team, our belief is when someone learns how to make peace with their past and let go of the insecurity and the triggers from their past, they will begin to see themselves blossom and learn to feel secure with who they are. Through the process, they will die to their old selves, patterns, habits, and will learn to become a radiant and secure person. They will take back the power from those who have projected wrong thinking on them. You will no longer wonder, "Will the Real Me Please Stand Up."

My final challenge is for you to love that person staring back at you in the mirror. Why? Because she/he wants to be your best friend 365 days a year, 7 days a week, 24 hours a day, until death do you part. Your REAL self wants to laugh with you, dance with you, dream with you.

Final scripture for you – Philippians 3:13 says, "Brothers and sisters, I do not consider myself yet to have taken hold of it. But one thing I do; forgetting what is behind and straining toward what is ahead." **You Can Do It, I Believe in You.**

Please stay in touch with me and let me know how you are doing.

To God Be the Glory

Tips from Terri

- Value yourself and put your needs first.

- Do positive self-talk every day until you believe it.

- Practice gratitude/give thanks.

- Get to know the REAL you.

- Do something every day that you enjoy.

- Love that person staring back at you in the mirror.

Imaginary Steps to See God Face to Face

When I want to see my Heavenly Father, this is the imaginary journey I take and I am inviting you to go on it with me.

*Please **close** your eyes and imagine yourself running through a long hallway where you can leave the world behind with all the problems we face every day.*

You see this big white door and you open it, and much to your amazement, it is absolutely breathtaking. It is a crystal blue sky day, there are rainbows, beautiful flowers, and flowing fountains. You see a narrow path with beautiful shaped hedges and water on each side of the path. You stop, and in a short distance, you see God. He motions you to come to Him with open arms. You run as fast as you can and jump into His arms.

You are anxious to tell your Heavenly Father everything about your day. But first, you tell Him how much you love and adore Him. Then, you share with Him your concerns, fears, struggles, hardships, and prayers for loved ones. You are REAL and you pour your heart out to Him. This is while He is holding onto you.

It is time to say goodbye and go back into the world. You stand up. God stands up and you touch His face and you say, I will see you tomorrow. I love you.

My friends, you just saw God face to face in an imaginary way because we all know we will truly see Him when we get to Heaven.

Psalms 27:8

Exodus 33:11

About the Author

Terri L. Moore is a motivational and dynamic keynote speaker, breakthrough, and vision coach. In personal empowerment sessions and motivational/inspirational events, Terri shares stories from her past about overcoming many challenges, setbacks, wounds, and failures. She will share her journey how she broke through barriers to find her true self, and identify her personal vision, to provide a road map for others to do the same.

Terri entered into a relationship with God when she was in her early thirties. She found God after going through much turmoil and trauma. She has been a strong Christian for over twenty-years. She loves God with all of her heart, soul, mind, and strength. Terri is also known as a prayer warrior.

Terri has accomplished much in her life. She became a semi-professional ice skater at the age of 17. Terri co-founded a domestic violence organization in 2007 and became the first executive director for six years. Terri also had the distinct honor to share the stage with Christian artist, Casting Crowns, to deliver a message of hope and healing to over 4,000 people. Terri is the CEO/founder of Terri L. Moore & Team, who serves women, men, and teens escaping from their past and find their beautiful vision.

Terri is available as a keynote and guest speaker, individual and group breakthrough and vision coaching sessions. Also, corporate and organizational team building, coaching, and workshops. Terri is available for ministerial and religious based team building and coaching. She has the experience to coach and speak on sexual assault and domestic violence abuse. She is available for seminars, and workshops, for large or small groups. Terri also provides internet coaching.

Terri is happily married to her husband, Scott, for over 20 years. She has one daughter, Lauren, two wonderful grandchildren, Bradyn and Zoey, and two fur babies Lilly and Max.

Find out more about Terri L. Moore
TERRI L. MOORE & TEAM, LLC
Phone # 317-201-8389
terri@terrilmooreandteam.com
www.TerriLMooreandTeam.Com
Like us on Facebook at *Face.com/terrilmooreandteam*

Twitter and LinkedIn

Inserts

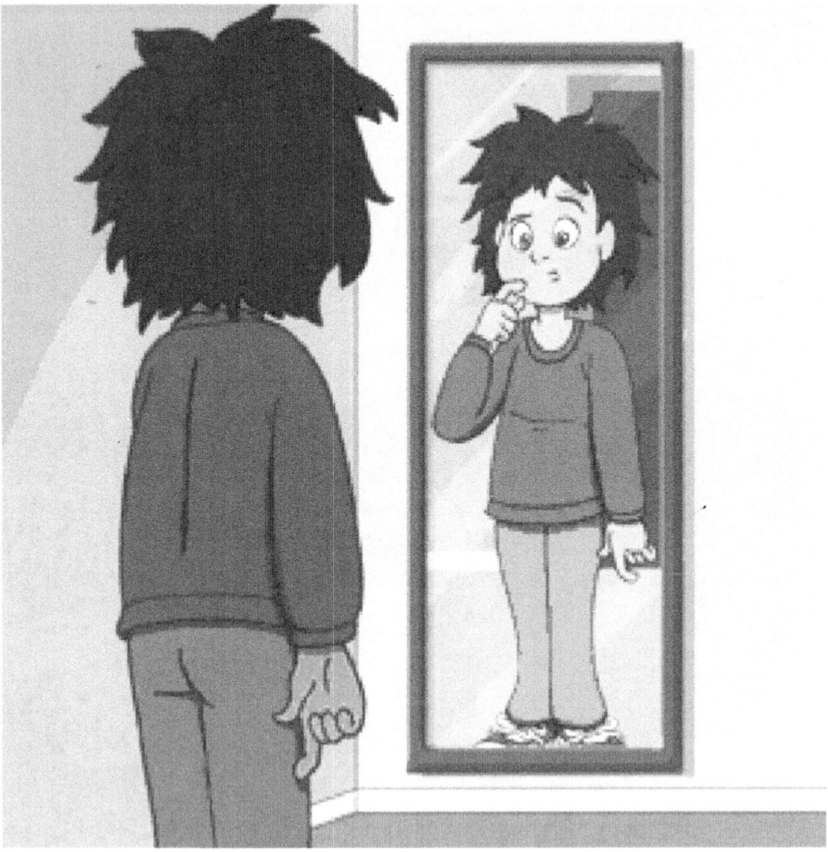

Negative Emotions List

- Abusive
- **Aggressive**
- **Angry**
- **Annoyed**
- Antagonistic
- **Anxious**
- **Arrogant**
- **Ashamed**
- Belligerent
- **Bitter**
- **Bored**
- Broken down
- Bullied
- Chaotic
- **Cold**
- **Commanding**
- Competitive
- Complaining
- **Conceited**
- Cruel
- Defeated
- Deluded
- **Demanding**
- Dependent
- Depressed
- Desperate
- Destitute
- Destructive
- Detached
- Disconnected
- **Discouraged**
- **Disgusted**
- **Dominated**
- **Dominating**
- Egocentric
- Egotistical
- Envious
- Erratic
- **Impatient**
- Impoverished
- **Impulsive**
- **Indifferent**
- Inert
- **Insecure**
- **Insensitive**
- Irresponsible
- **Irritated**
- Isolated
- Jealous
- **Judged**
- **Judgmental**
- Lazy
- Lonely
- Lost
- **Mad**
- **Manipulated**
- **Manipulative**

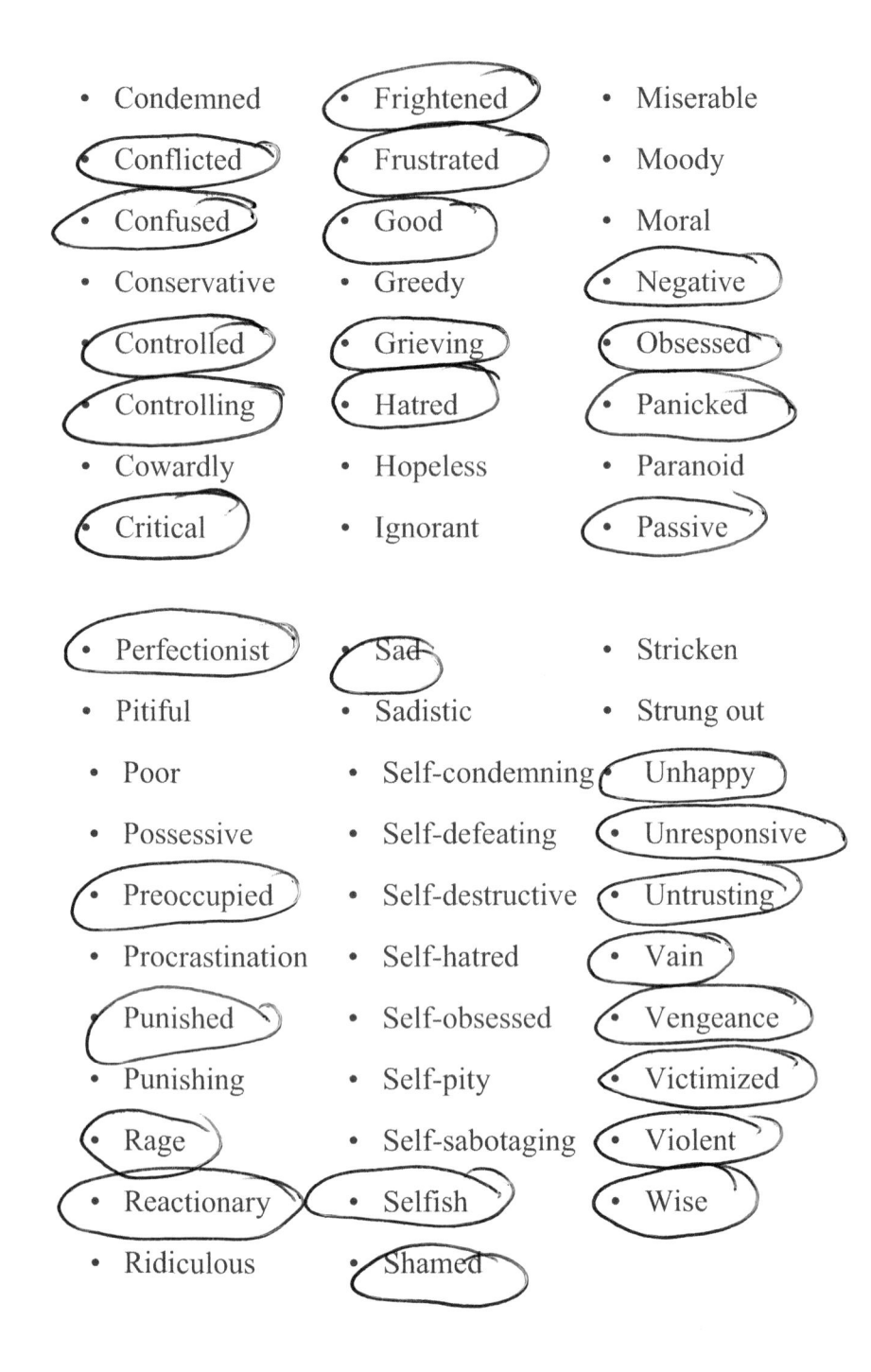

- Condemned
- Conflicted
- Confused
- Conservative
- Controlled
- Controlling
- Cowardly
- Critical

- Frightened
- Frustrated
- Good
- Greedy
- Grieving
- Hatred
- Hopeless
- Ignorant

- Miserable
- Moody
- Moral
- Negative
- Obsessed
- Panicked
- Paranoid
- Passive

- Perfectionist
- Pitiful
- Poor
- Possessive
- Preoccupied
- Procrastination
- Punished
- Punishing
- Rage
- Reactionary
- Ridiculous

- Sad
- Sadistic
- Self-condemning
- Self-defeating
- Self-destructive
- Self-hatred
- Self-obsessed
- Self-pity
- Self-sabotaging
- Selfish
- Shamed

- Stricken
- Strung out
- Unhappy
- Unresponsive
- Untrusting
- Vain
- Vengeance
- Victimized
- Violent
- Wise

- (Righteous)
- Ruthless
- Shut down
- (Sorry)

Positive Emotions List

- Accountable
- Adaptable
- Adventurous
- Alert
- Ambitious
- Appropriate
- Assertive
- Astute
- Attentive
- Authentic
- Aware
- Bravery
- Calm
- Candid
- Capable
- Certain
- Charismatic
- Clear
- Collaborative
- Consistent
- Contributes
- Cooperative
- Courageous
- Creative
- Curious
- Dedicated
- Determined
- Diplomatic
- Directive
- Disciplined
- Dynamic
- Easygoing
- Effective
- Efficient
- Empathetic
- Empowers
- Energetic
- Enthusiastic
- Flexible
- Friendly
- Generative
- Generosity
- Gratitude
- Happy
- Hard Working
- Honest
- Honorable
- Humorous
- Imaginative
- Immaculate
- Independent
- Initiates
- Innovative
- Inquiring
- Intentional
- Interested
- Intimate

- Committed
- Communicator
- Compassion
- Comradeship
- Connected
- Conscious
- Considerate

- Ethical
- Excited
- Expressive
- Facilitates
- Fairness
- Faithful
- Fearless

- Joyful
- Knowledgeable
- Leading
- Listener
- Lively
- Logical
- Loving

- Loyal
- Manages Time Well
- Networker
- Nurturing
- Open-Minded
- Optimism
- Organized
- Patient
- Peaceful
- Planner
- Playful

- Presents Self Well
- Proactive
- Problem-Solver
- Productive
- Punctual
- Reliable
- Resourceful
- Responsible
- Self-confident
- Self-generating
- Self-reliant

- Spiritual
- Spontaneous
- Stable
- Strong
- Successful
- Supportive
- Tactful
- Trusting
- Trustworthy
- Truthful
- Versatile

- Poised
- Polite
- Powerful
- Practical

- Sense of Humor
- Sensual
- Serves Others
- Sincere
- Skillful

- Vibrant
- Warm
- Willing
- Wise
- Zealous

Made in the USA
Monee, IL
01 July 2021